The UNAUTHORIZED

Beanie Baby Guide

Not associated with or sponsored by the makers of Beanie Babies©

by Lee Dralle & Lynn Dralle Wilson

SCHOLASTIC INC.

New York Toronto London Auckland Sydney
Mexico City New Delhi Hong Kong

Copyright © 1998 Lee Dralle & Lynn Dralle Wilson
All rights reserved. Published by Scholastic Inc.
SCHOLASTIC and associated logos are trademarks and/or registered trademarks of Scholastic Inc.

TY, BEANIE BABIES, and BEANIE BABIES COLLECTION are registered trademarks of Ty Inc.

Beanies pictured courtesy of Cheryl Leaf, Cindy Harris, Pam Alderson, Jill Blair, Heather Ekland, Alex Lihou, Linda Gallagher, Melissa Bruce, Tracey & Tamir, Peggy Mohr, Kim Barlow & Frank Falgiani . . .
Thanks!

Clubby: copyright, USA TODAY. Reprinted with permission.

ISBN 0-590-63478-X

12 11 10 9 8 7 6 5 4 3 2   8 9/9 0 1 2 3/0
Printed in the U.S.A.

First Scholastic printing, November 1998

To contact the authors, please write to:
a.k.a. publishing, Inc.
2828 Northwest Ave.
Bellingham, WA 98225
akapress@pacificrim.net

This Book is Dedicated to:
CHERYL LEAF
The World's Best Grandmother

Our Greatest Thanks to Bonnie Bader and Scholastic,
Kristin Earhart, Madalina Stefan, Linda Lewis, Jon Brunk,
Cheryl Leaf, Wayne & Sue Dralle, William & Houston Wilson,
Kristin Dralle, Sharon Chase, and, of course, Ty Inc.

Table of Contents

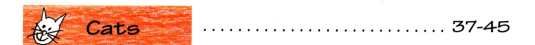

Bernie, Bones, Bruno, Doby, Dotty, Fetch, Gigi, Nanook, Pugsly, Rover, Scottie, Sparky, Spot, Spunky, Tracker, Tuffy, Weenie, Wrinkles

Chip, Flip, Nip, Nip with white face, Pounce, Prance, Snip, Zip, Zip with white face

Collecting Is Fun!

My brother, Lee, and I started collecting things when we were very young. Lee collected Canadian silver dollars, bells with animals on them, and choo choo trains. I collected Canadian silver dollars, silver napkin rings, bells with people on them, and Abraham Lincoln items (he was my favorite president!). Even though we began collecting when we were just tiny, we still have most of our collections and treasure them to this day. Our collections turned out to be good investments, also. In fact, the Canadian silver dollars helped pay for both of our college educations. Here we are with some of our first collections.

How did we get into collecting in the first place? Well, our grandmother Cheryl Leaf (who happens to own an antique and gift store) began teaching us about antiques and collecting when we were little kids. She taught us how to hunt for bargains in any store in the world. She says that no matter where you are you can find a treasure if you just apply yourself. She also took us on many trips around the world. From a very young age we were able to hunt items for our collections in such fun places as Europe, Hong Kong, and Mexico. And from then on, we were hooked!

We still help our grandmother (who is 86 years old) with her business. It was in our grandmother's store that we first saw those adorable Ty Beanie Babies®and began collecting them. Here is our grandma holding a bunch of Beanie Babies®.

BEAN THERE: Cheryl Leaf, 85, holds Beanie Babies, one of the hot items to give as gifts this year. Leaf is the original owner of Cheryl Leaf Antiques & Gifts, which she has owned for 47 years.

We have seen a lot of fads come and go, but we feel (and you probably do, too) that the Beanie Baby craze is here to stay! We hope you have as much fun collecting and keeping track of your Beanie Babies®as we do.

Lee (age 3)   Lynn (age 6)

How to Use This Book

Each Beanie has its own page:

There is a page for each official Ty Beanie that has been produced up through July 1998. Sometimes there are two variations of a Beanie on one page. For example, Spot with a spot and Spot without a spot appear on the same page.

Write your info on each page:

Each page has a place for you to keep track of when you got the Beanie, how much you paid for it or who gave it to you, plus there is room for you to write special notes about each Beanie. Also listed are the Beanies' birthdays, introduction dates, and retired dates. If a Beanie hasn't been retired, there is a blank line for you to fill in the date when it is retired.

Market values:

Market values — how much the Beanie is worth today and how much we think it will be worth 10 years from now — are also listed. Remember that values are for Beanies with perfect condition hang tags. Take 25% off for a bent tag and 50% off for no tag. **The prices listed are just estimated guidelines and are not guaranteed in any way.** (In the book, "est." stands for estimated.)

This book is sorted by animal type:

This book is sorted by dogs, cats, farm animals, jungle animals, forest animals, sea life, crawlers, bears, animals with wings, make-believe, dinosaurs, and patriotic. If you're not sure which category your Beanie falls under, then check out the index at the back of the book.

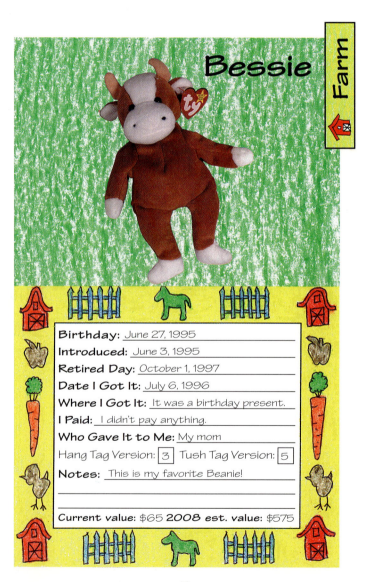

Bessie

Farm

Birthday: June 27, 1995

Introduced: June 3, 1995

Retired Day: October 1, 1997

Date I Got It: July 6, 1996

Where I Got It: It was a birthday present.

I Paid: I didn't pay anything.

Who Gave It to Me: My mom

Hang Tag Version: 3 | Tush Tag Version: 5

Notes: This is my favorite Beanie!

Current value: $65 **2008 est. value:** $575

HANG TAGS

The hang tag is very important to a serious collector. A Beanie Baby with a perfect hang tag can be worth twice as much as one with no tag at all. A tag in perfect condition has no creases and no worn areas where white shows through the red. Creases, tears, and worn areas will lower the value of the Beanie Baby about 25%.

The first version of the hang tag was used on the very first Beanies and the fifth used on Beanies being made when this book went to press.

1st Version:
This tag does not open. It is a single heart with a skinny "ty" printed on it. Beanie style number and name are printed on the back.

2nd Version:
The front of this tag is just like the 1st version, only now it opens like a book. The tag has the Beanie style number and name printed on the inside. Some have "TO:_____ FROM: _____ with LOVE."

3rd Version:
This tag still opens like a book and includes the Beanie style number and name. The "ty" is now more rounded. Some still have "TO: _____ FROM: _____ with LOVE."

4th Version:
This tag is the same as the 3rd version but with an added yellow star that says "BEANIE ORIGINAL BABY." No more TO/FROM. Poems and date of birth have been added.

5th Version:
The typeface of this tag is similar to the 4th version. This tag's main differences are a new typeface on the inside and in the star on the front, no Beanie style number, and the birthdays are written in longhand — for example, November 20, 1997 instead of 11-20-97.

It's important to protect your hang tags. There are many companies selling tag protectors to help keep your Beanies' tags in perfect condition.

TUSH TAGS

Tush tags are cloth tags sewn into a seam of the Beanie toward the rear. The type of tush tag will give a general idea of when the Beanie was produced. The six types of tags were produced in the order shown here.

© 1993 TY INC.,	ALL NEW MATERIAL
OAKBROOK IL.U.S.A.	POLYESTER FIBER
ALL RIGHTS RESERVED	& P.V.C. PELLETS
HANDMADE IN CHINA	PA. REG #1965
SURFACE WASHABLE	FOR AGES 3 AND UP

1st Version:

This is a black-and-white cloth tag with no Beanie name.

2nd Version:

This is a red-and-white cloth tag with no Beanie name. It features the red "ty" heart.

3rd Version:

This is also a red-and-white cloth tag but now the name of the Beanie Baby appears on it. The red words "The Beanie Babies Collection™" appear on this tag above the smaller red "ty" heart.

4th Version:

This tag is very similar to the red-and-white 3rd version tag, only now a red star appears to the left of the "ty" heart. Some 4th version tags are actually 3rd version tags with a plastic red star stuck on it.

5th Version:
The only changes between
this version and the 4th
version are the ™ symbol added
to the Beanie's name and
an ® added after Beanie Babies.

6th Version:
This tag is similar to the 5th version,
however there are now two ® marks.
One of the ® marks has been moved to
the end of "The Beanie Babies
Collection," but the other ®
is still by the heart.

Bernie™
the St. Bernard

BOW

Birthday: _October 3, 1996_

Introduced: _January 1, 1997_

Retired Day: _____

Date I Got It: _____

Where I Got It: _____

I Paid: $ _____ _or_

Who Gave It to Me: _____

Hang Tag Version: ☐   Tush Tag Version: ☐

Notes: _____
_____
_____

Current value: $12   2008 est. value: $195

WOW

PUPPY   PUPPY

Bones™
the Dog

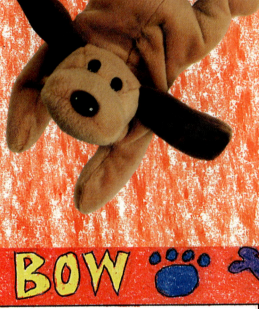

BOW

Birthday: _____ January 18, 1994 _____

Introduced: _____ June 25, 1994 _____

Retired Day: _____ May 1, 1998 _____

Date I Got It: _____

Where I Got It: _____

I Paid: $ _____ **or**

Who Gave It to Me: _____

Hang Tag Version: ☐   Tush Tag Version: ☐

Notes: _____
_____
_____

Current value: **$25**   2008 est. value: **$275**

WOW

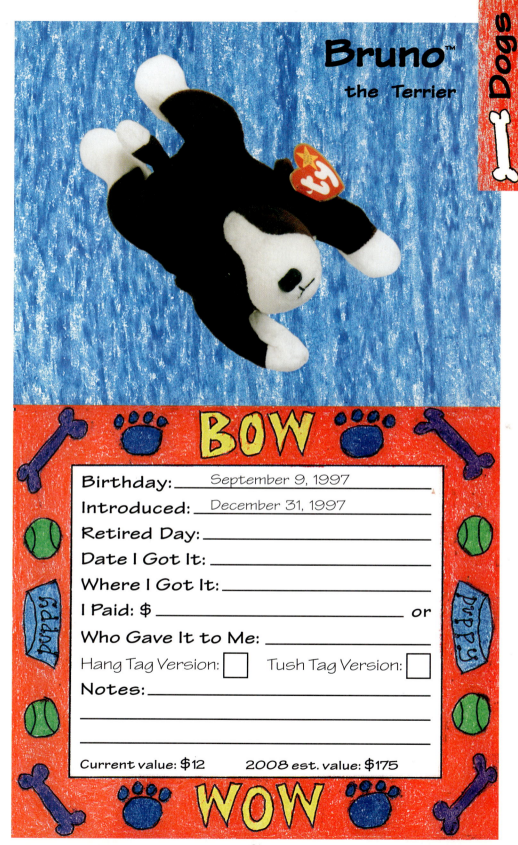

Bruno™
the Terrier

BOW

Birthday: September 9, 1997

Introduced: December 31, 1997

Retired Day: _____

Date I Got It: _____

Where I Got It: _____

I Paid: $ _____ or

Who Gave It to Me: _____

Hang Tag Version: ☐   Tush Tag Version: ☐

Notes: _____

_____

_____

Current value: $12   2008 est. value: $175

WOW

PUPPY   PUPPY

Doby™
the Doberman

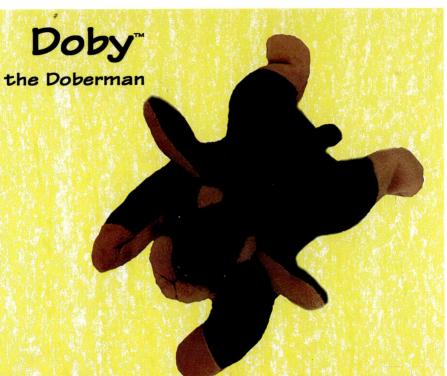

BOW

Birthday: _____October 9, 1996_____

Introduced: _____January 1, 1997_____

Retired Day: _____

Date I Got It: _____

Where I Got It: _____

I Paid: $ _____ or

Who Gave It to Me: _____

Hang Tag Version: ☐   Tush Tag Version: ☐

Notes: _____

_____

_____

Current value: $12   2008 est. value: $175

WOW

Dotty™
the Dalmatian

Dogs

BOW

Birthday: October 17, 1996

Introduced: May 11, 1997

Retired Day: _____

Date I Got It: _____

Where I Got It: _____

I Paid: $ _____ or

Who Gave It to Me: _____

Hang Tag Version: ☐   Tush Tag Version: ☐

Notes: _____

_____

_____

Current value: $12   2008 est. value: $195

WOW

PUPPY

PUPPY

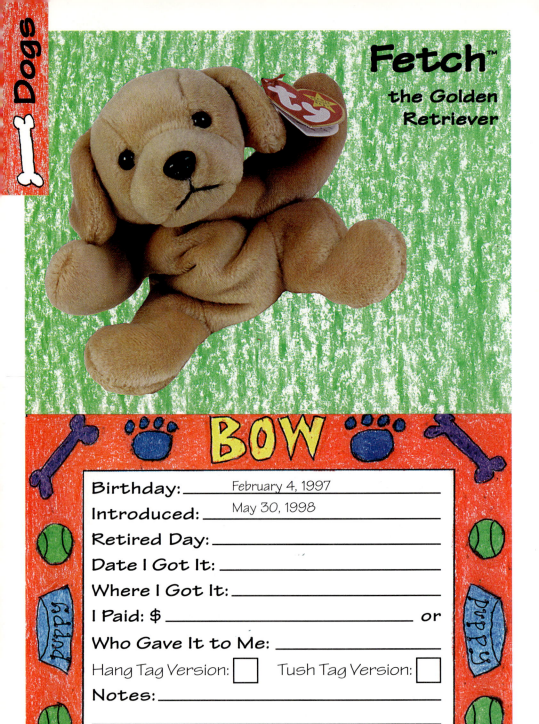

Fetch™
the Golden Retriever

BOW

Birthday:	February 4, 1997
Introduced:	May 30, 1998
Retired Day:	
Date I Got It:	
Where I Got It:	
I Paid: $	or
Who Gave It to Me:	

Hang Tag Version: ☐   Tush Tag Version: ☐

Notes:

Current value: $12   2008 est. value: $185

WOW

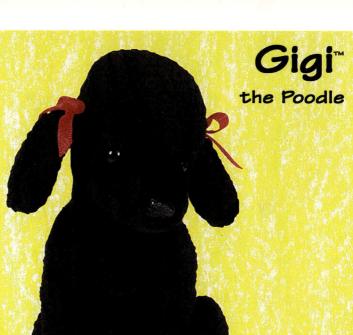

Gigi™
the Poodle

BOW

Birthday: _April 7, 1997_

Introduced: _May 30, 1998_

Retired Day: _____

Date I Got It: _March 10, 1999_

Where I Got It: _My Birthday-10th_

I Paid: $ _____ or

Who Gave It to Me: _Mommy_

Hang Tag Version: ☐   Tush Tag Version: ☐

Notes: _____

_____

_____

Current value: $12   2008 est. value: $225

WOW

Nanook™
the Husky

BOW

Birthday: November 21, 1996

Introduced: May 11, 1997

Retired Day: _____

Date I Got It: _March 11, 1999_

Where I Got It: _My Birthday_

I Paid: $ _____ or

Who Gave It to Me: _____

Hang Tag Version: ☐   Tush Tag Version: ☐

Notes: _____
_____
_____

Current value: $15   2008 est. value: $245

WOW

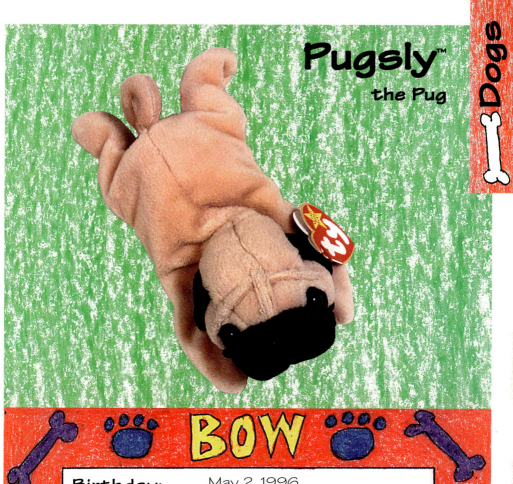

Dogs

Pugsly™
the Pug

BOW

Birthday: _May 2, 1996_

Introduced: _May 11, 1997_

Retired Day: _____

Date I Got It: _____

Where I Got It: _____

I Paid: $ _____ or

Who Gave It to Me: _____

Hang Tag Version: ☐   Tush Tag Version: ☐

Notes: _____

_____

_____

Current value: $12   2008 est. value: $195

WOW

PUPPY   PUPPY

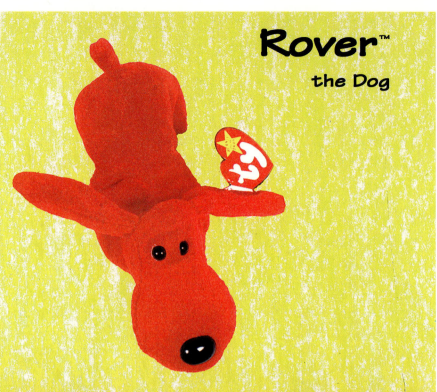

Rover™
the Dog

BOW

Birthday: May 30, 1996

Introduced: June 15, 1996

Retired Day: May 1, 1998

Date I Got It: _____

Where I Got It: _____

I Paid: $ _____ or

Who Gave It to Me: _____

Hang Tag Version: ☐   Tush Tag Version: ☐

Notes: _____

_____

_____

Current value: **$35**   2008 est. value: **$295**

WOW

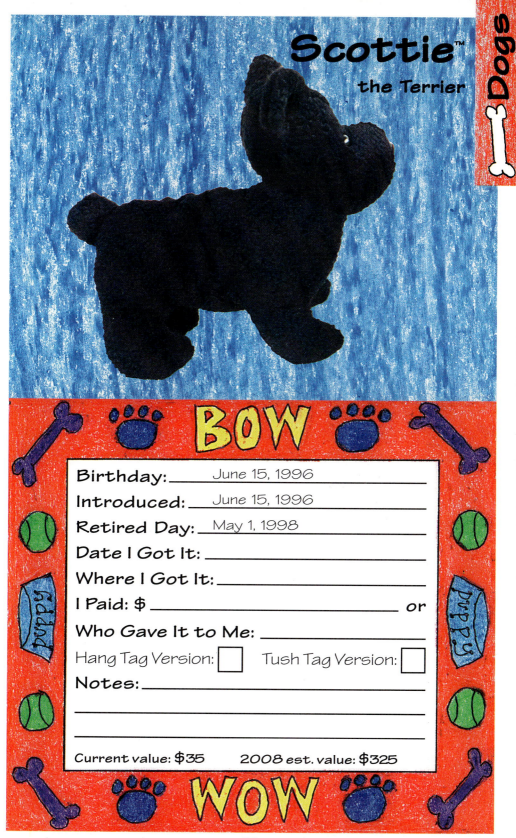

Scottie™
the Terrier

Dogs

BOW

Birthday: _____ June 15, 1996 _____

Introduced: _____ June 15, 1996 _____

Retired Day: _____ May 1, 1998 _____

Date I Got It: _____

Where I Got It: _____

I Paid: $ _____ or

Who Gave It to Me: _____

Hang Tag Version: ☐   Tush Tag Version: ☐

Notes: _____

_____

_____

Current value: $35   2008 est. value: $325

PUPPY

PUPPY

WOW

Sparky™
the Dalmatian

BOW

Birthday: February 27, 1996

Introduced: June 15, 1996

Retired Day: May 11, 1997

Date I Got It: _____

Where I Got It: _____

I Paid: $ _____ or

Who Gave It to Me: _____

Hang Tag Version: ☐   Tush Tag Version: ☐

Notes: _____
_____
_____

Current value: $145   2008 est. value: $425

PUPPY   PUPPY

WOW

Spot™

the Dog
without &
with a spot

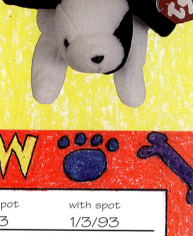

BOW

	without spot	with spot
Birthday:	1/3/93	1/3/93
Introduced:	1/8/94	4/13/94
Retired Day:	4/13/94	10/1/97

Date I Got It: _____

Where I Got It: _____

I Paid: $ _____ or

Who Gave It to Me: _____

Hang Tag Version: ☐   Tush Tag Version: ☐

Notes: _____

Current value:

  $65 with spot

  $2250 without spot

2008 est. value:

  $395 with spot

  $2750 without spot

puppy

puppy

WOW

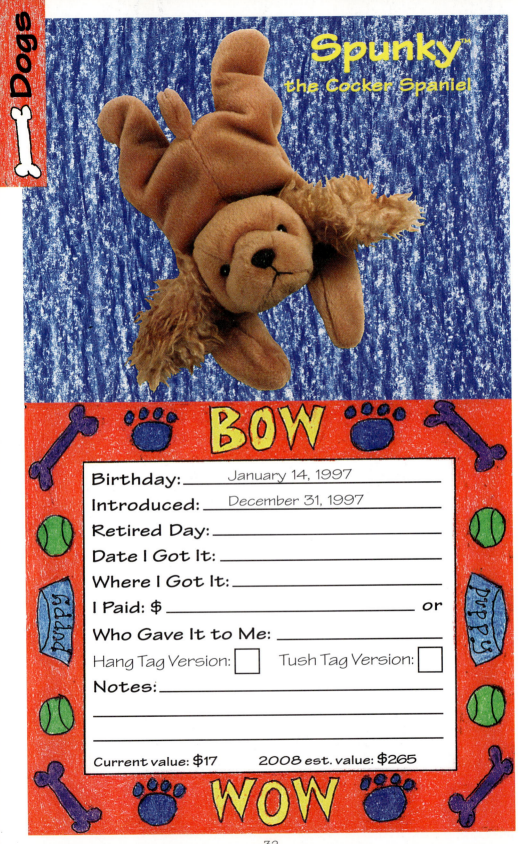

Spunky™
the Cocker Spaniel

BOW

Birthday: _January 14, 1997_

Introduced: _December 31, 1997_

Retired Day: _____

Date I Got It: _____

Where I Got It: _____

I Paid: $ _____ or

Who Gave It to Me: _____

Hang Tag Version: ☐   Tush Tag Version: ☐

Notes: _____

_____

_____

Current value: $17   2008 est. value: $265

WOW

32

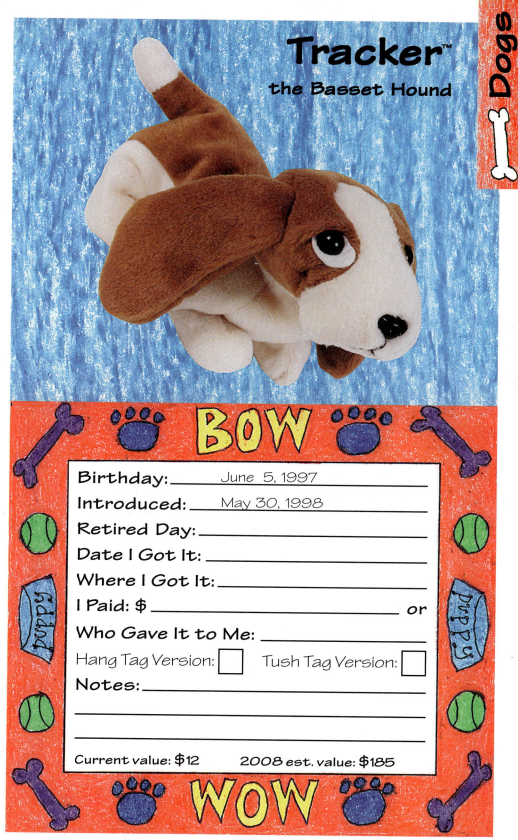

Tracker™
the Basset Hound

BOW

Birthday: June 5, 1997

Introduced: May 30, 1998

Retired Day: _____

Date I Got It: _____

Where I Got It: _____

I Paid: $ _____ **or**

Who Gave It to Me: _____

Hang Tag Version: ☐   Tush Tag Version: ☐

Notes: _____

_____

_____

Current value: $12   2008 est. value: $185

puppy

puppy

WOW

Tuffy™
the Terrier

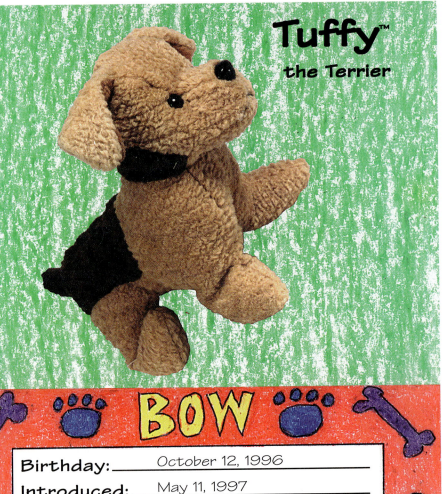

BOW

Birthday: _October 12, 1996_

Introduced: _May 11, 1997_

Retired Day: _____

Date I Got It: _____

Where I Got It: _____

I Paid: $ _____ or

Who Gave It to Me: _____

Hang Tag Version: ☐   Tush Tag Version: ☐

Notes: _____

_____

_____

Current value: **$15**   2008 est. value: **$235**

WOW

Weenie™
the Dachshund

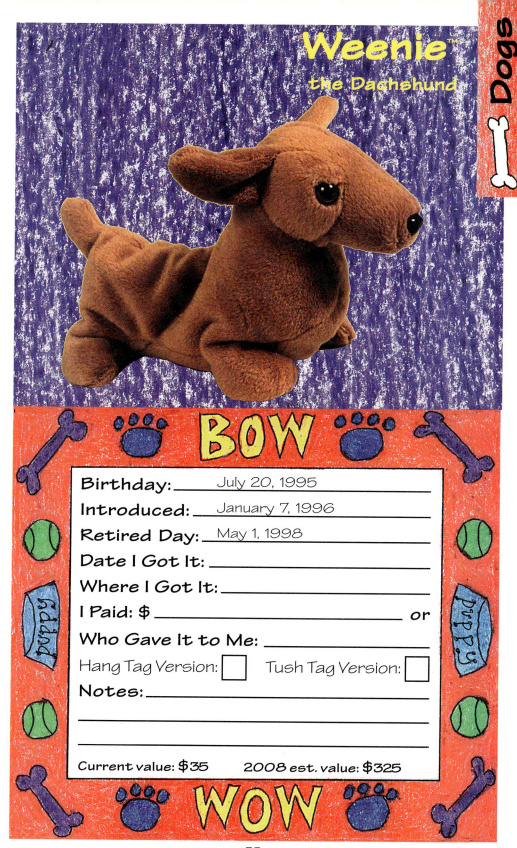

BOW

Birthday: _July 20, 1995_

Introduced: _January 7, 1996_

Retired Day: _May 1, 1998_

Date I Got It: _____

Where I Got It: _____

I Paid: $ _____ **or**

Who Gave It to Me: _____

Hang Tag Version: ☐   Tush Tag Version: ☐

Notes: _____
_____
_____

Current value: **$35**   2008 est. value: **$325**

WOW

Wrinkles™
the Bulldog

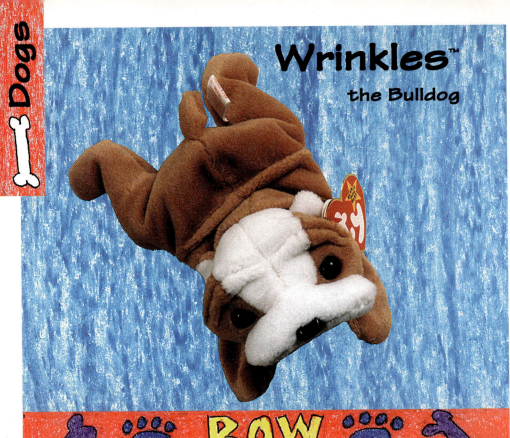

BOW

Birthday: _May 1, 1996_

Introduced: _June 15, 1996_

Retired Day: _____

Date I Got It: _____

Where I Got It: _____

I Paid: $ _____ or

Who Gave It to Me: _____

Hang Tag Version: ☐   Tush Tag Version: ☐

Notes: _____
_____
_____

Current value: $12   **2008 est. value: $185**

WOW

Chip™
the Calico Cat

MEOW

Birthday: _January 26, 1996_

Introduced: _May 11, 1997_

Retired Day: _____

Date I Got It: _____

Where I Got It: _____

I Paid: $ _____ or

Who Gave It to Me: _____

Hang Tag Version: ☐   Tush Tag Version: ☐

Notes: _____

_____

_____

Current value: **$12**   2008 est. value: **$225**

MEOW

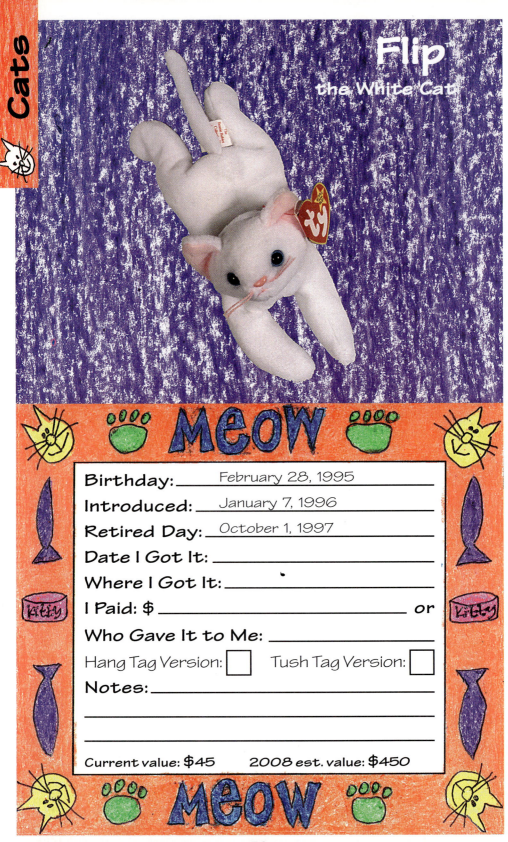

Flip
the White Cat

MEOW

Birthday: February 28, 1995

Introduced: January 7, 1996

Retired Day: October 1, 1997

Date I Got It: _____

Where I Got It: _____

I Paid: $ _____ or

Who Gave It to Me: _____

Hang Tag Version: ☐   **Tush Tag Version:** ☐

Notes: _____
_____
_____

Current value: **$45**   2008 est. value: **$450**

MEOW

Nip™
the Gold Cat
with white paws
& all gold

MEOW

	with white paws	all gold
Birthday:	3/6/94	3/6/94
Introduced:	3/10/96	1/7/96
Retired Day:	12/31/97	3/10/96

Date I Got It: _____

Where I Got It: _____

I Paid: $ _____ or

Who Gave It to Me: _____

Hang Tag Version: ☐   Tush Tag Version: ☐

Notes: _____

Current value:
   $35 with white paws
   $925 all gold

2008 est. value:
   $295 with white paws
   $1500 all gold

kitty   kitty

MEOW

Nip™
the Gold Cat
with white face

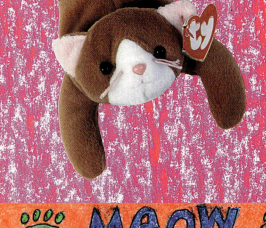

MEOW

Birthday: _March 6, 1994_

Introduced: _January 7, 1995_

Retired Day: _January 7, 1996_

Date I Got It: _____

Where I Got It: _____

I Paid: $ _____ or

Who Gave It to Me: _____

Hang Tag Version: ☐   Tush Tag Version: ☐

Notes: _____
_____
_____

Current value: **$585**   2008 est. value: **$1275**

MEOW

Pounce™
the Cat

MEOW

Birthday: August 28, 1997

Introduced: December 31, 1997

Retired Day: _____

Date I Got It: _____

Where I Got It: _____

I Paid: $ _____ or

Who Gave It to Me: _____

Hang Tag Version: ☐   Tush Tag Version: ☐

Notes: _____

_____

_____

Current value: **$12**   2008 est. value: **$195**

MEOW

Prance™
the Cat

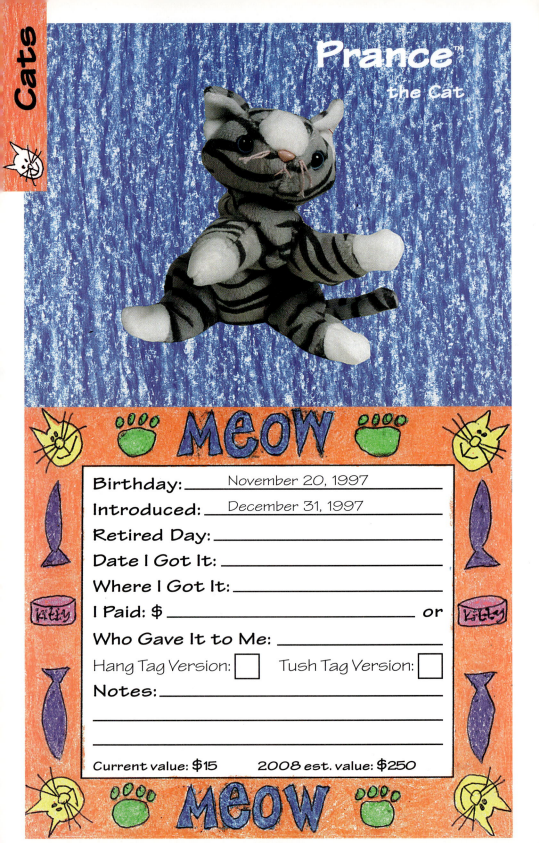

MEOW

Birthday: _November 20, 1997_

Introduced: _December 31, 1997_

Retired Day: _____

Date I Got It: _____

Where I Got It: _____

I Paid: $ _____ **or**

Who Gave It to Me: _____

Hang Tag Version: ☐   Tush Tag Version: ☐

Notes: _____
_____
_____

Current value: **$15**   2008 est. value: **$250**

MEOW

42

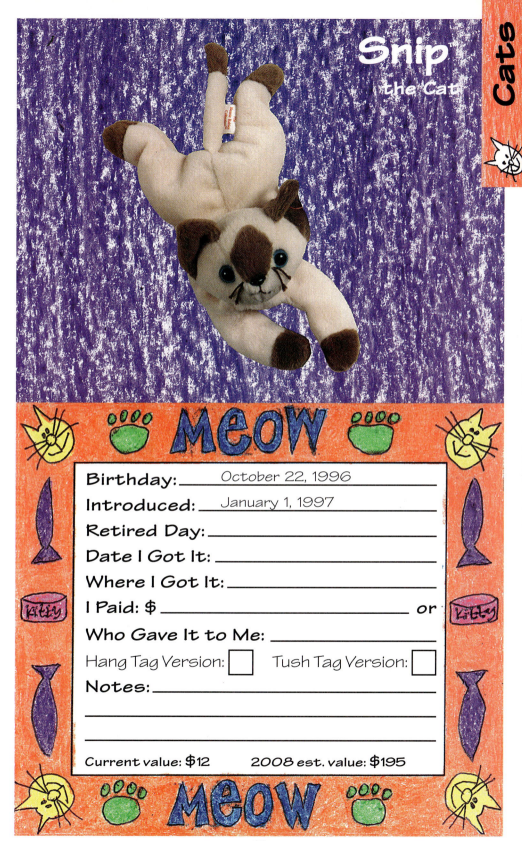

Snip™ the Cat

MEOW

Birthday: October 22, 1996

Introduced: January 1, 1997

Retired Day: _____

Date I Got It: _____

Where I Got It: _____

I Paid: $ _____ or

Who Gave It to Me: _____

Hang Tag Version: ☐   Tush Tag Version: ☐

Notes: _____
_____
_____

Current value: $12   2008 est. value: $195

MEOW

Zip™

the Black Cat
with white paws
& all black

MEOW

	with white paws	all black
Birthday:	3/28/94	3/28/94
Introduced:	3/10/96	1/7/96
Retired Day:	5/1/98	3/10/96

Date I Got It: _____

Where I Got It: _____

I Paid: $ _____ or

Who Gave It to Me: _____

Hang Tag Version: ☐   Tush Tag Version: ☐

Notes: _____

Current value:
   $55 with white paws
   $2000 all black

2008 est. value:
   $595 with white paws
   $2850 all black

MEOW

Zip™
the Black Cat
with the white face

MEOW

Birthday: _____ March 28, 1994 _____

Introduced: _____ January 7, 1995 _____

Retired Day: _____ January 7, 1996 _____

Date I Got It: _____

Where I Got It: _____

I Paid: $ _____ or

Who Gave It to Me: _____

Hang Tag Version: ☐   Tush Tag Version: ☐

Notes: _____

_____

_____

Current value: $575   2008 est. value: $1285

MEOW

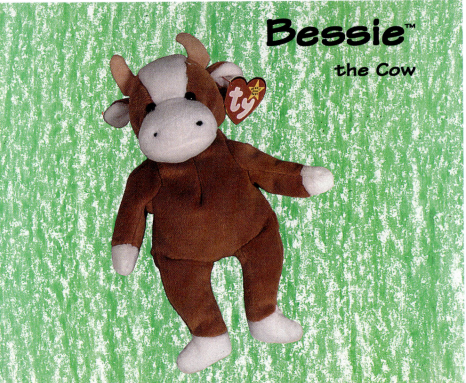

Bessie™

the Cow

Birthday: _June 27, 1995_

Introduced: _June 3, 1995_

Retired Day: _October 1, 1997_

Date I Got It: _____

Where I Got It: _____

I Paid: $ _____ or

Who Gave It to Me: _____

Hang Tag Version: ☐   Tush Tag Version: ☐

Notes: _____
_____
_____

Current value: $65   2008 est. value: $575

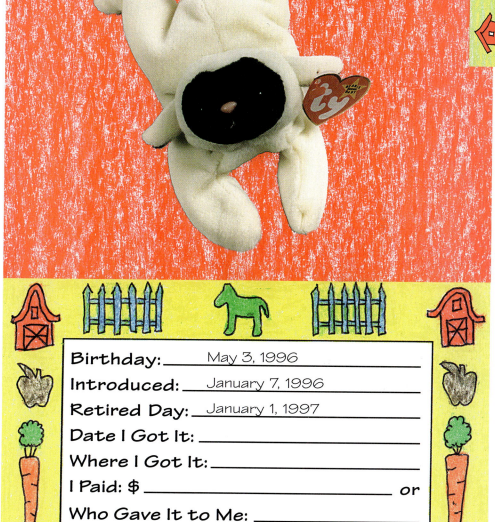

Chops™
the Lamb

Birthday: _May 3, 1996_

Introduced: _January 7, 1996_

Retired Day: _January 1, 1997_

Date I Got It: _____

Where I Got It: _____

I Paid: $ _____ or

Who Gave It to Me: _____

Hang Tag Version: ☐   Tush Tag Version: ☐

Notes: _____
_____
_____

Current value: $195   2008 est. value: $650

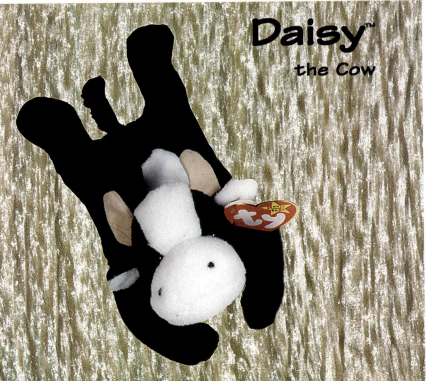

Daisy™
the Cow

Birthday: May 10, 1994

Introduced: June 25, 1994

Retired Day: _____

Date I Got It: _____

Where I Got It: _____

I Paid: $ _____ **or**

Who Gave It to Me: _____

Hang Tag Version: ☐   Tush Tag Version: ☐

Notes: _____
_____
_____

Current value: $12   2008 est. value: $225

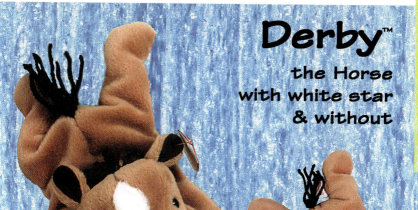

Derby™

the Horse
with white star
& without

	with white star	without white star
Birthday:	9/16/95	9/16/95
Introduced:	12/15/97	6/3/95
Retired Day:		12/15/97

Date I Got It: _____

Where I Got It: _____

I Paid: $ _____ or

Who Gave It to Me: _____

Hang Tag Version: ☐ Tush Tag Version: ☐

Notes: _____

Current value:	2008 est. value:
$15 w/ white star	$275 w/ white star
$35 w/o white star	$395 w/o white star

49

Fleece™
the Napped Lamb

Birthday: March 21, 1996

Introduced: January 1, 1997

Retired Day: _____

Date I Got It: _____

Where I Got It: _____

I Paid: $ _____ **or**

Who Gave It to Me: _____

Hang Tag Version: ☐   Tush Tag Version: ☐

Notes: _____
_____
_____

Current value: **$12**   2008 est. value: **$225**

Grunt™
the Razorback

Birthday: _July 19, 1995_

Introduced: _January 7, 1996_

Retired Day: _May 11, 1997_

Date I Got It: _____

Where I Got It: _____

I Paid: $ _____ or

Who Gave It to Me: _____

Hang Tag Version: ☐   Tush Tag Version: ☐

Notes: _____
_____
_____

Current value: **$185**   2008 est. value: **$525**

Farm

Quackers™

the Duck
wingless & with wings

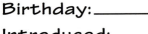

	wingless	with wings
Birthday:	4/19/94	4/19/94
Introduced:	6/25/94	1/7/95
Retired Day:	1/7/95	5/1/98

Date I Got It: _____

Where I Got It: _____

I Paid: $ _____ **or**

Who Gave It to Me: _____

Hang Tag Version: ☐   Tush Tag Version: ☐

Notes: _____

Current value: 2008 est. value:
  $2250 w/o wings $2950 w/o wings
  $25 w/ wings $245 w/ wings

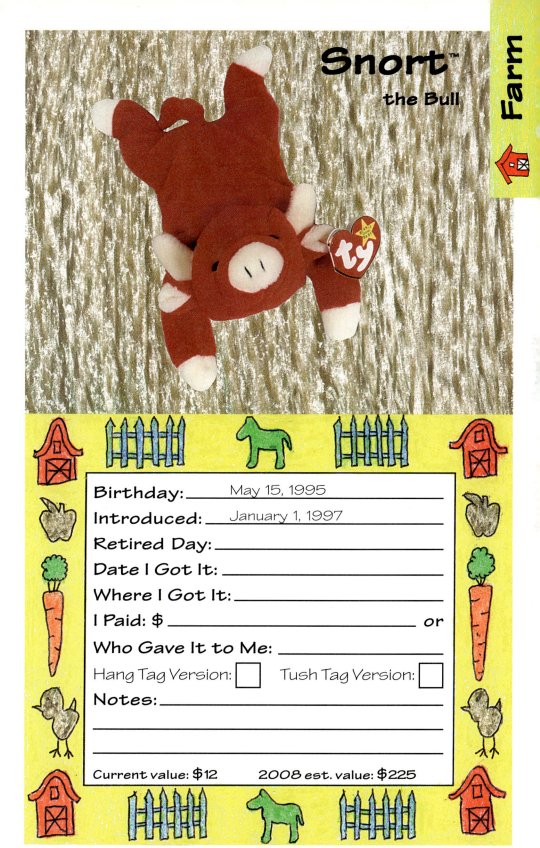

Snort™
the Bull

Farm

Birthday: May 15, 1995

Introduced: January 1, 1997

Retired Day: _____

Date I Got It: _____

Where I Got It: _____

I Paid: $ _____ or

Who Gave It to Me: _____

Hang Tag Version: ☐   Tush Tag Version: ☐

Notes: _____

_____

_____

Current value: $12   2008 est. value: $225

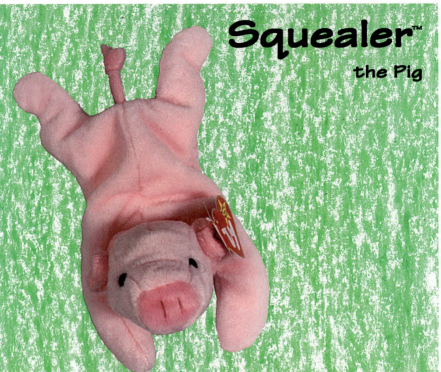

Squealer™
the Pig

Birthday: _____ April 23, 1993 _____

Introduced: _____ January 8, 1994 _____

Retired Day: _____ May 1, 1998 _____

Date I Got It: _____

Where I Got It: _____

I Paid: $ _____ or

Who Gave It to Me: _____

Hang Tag Version: ☐   Tush Tag Version: ☐

Notes: _____

_____

_____

Current value: $35   2008 est. value: $345

Strut™

the Rooster
(Formerly Doodle)

	Strut	Doodle
Birthday:	3/8/96	3/8/96
Introduced:	7/12/97	5/11/97
Retired Day:		7/12/97

Date I Got It: _____

Where I Got It: _____

I Paid: $ _____ or

Who Gave It to Me: _____

Hang Tag Version: ☐   Tush Tag Version: ☐

Notes: _____

Current value: 2008 est. value:
   $18 Strut $295 Strut
   $55 Doodle $535 Doodle

Tabasco™
the Bull

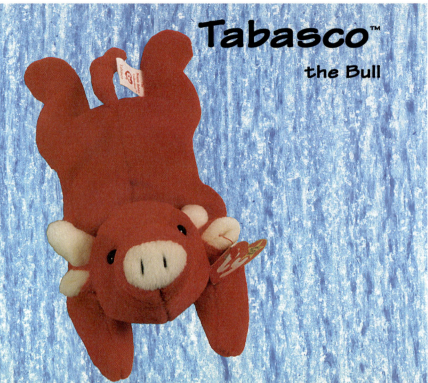

Birthday: _____ May 15, 1995 _____

Introduced: _____ June 3, 1995 _____

Retired Day: _____ January 1, 1997 _____

Date I Got It: _____

Where I Got It: _____

I Paid: $ _____ or

Who Gave It to Me: _____

Hang Tag Version: ☐   Tush Tag Version: ☐

Notes: _____

_____

_____

Current value: $225   2008 est. value: $650

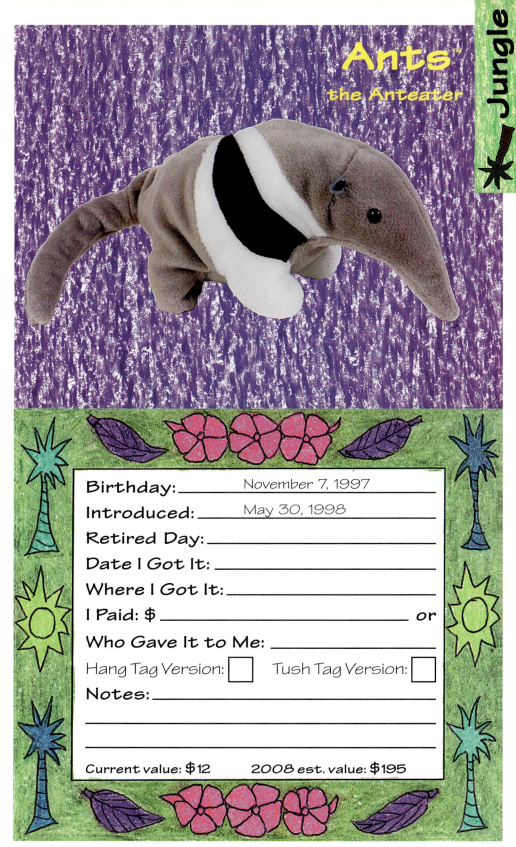

Ants™
the Anteater

Birthday: _____ November 7, 1997 _____

Introduced: _____ May 30, 1998 _____

Retired Day: _____

Date I Got It: _____

Where I Got It: _____

I Paid: $ _____ or

Who Gave It to Me: _____

Hang Tag Version: ☐   Tush Tag Version: ☐

Notes: _____

_____

_____

Current value: $12   2008 est. value: $195

Blizzard™
the Tiger

Birthday: ___December 12, 1996___

Introduced: ___May 11, 1997___

Retired Day: ___May 1, 1998___

Date I Got It: _____

Where I Got It: _____

I Paid: $ _____ or

Who Gave It to Me: _____

Hang Tag Version: ☐   Tush Tag Version: ☐

Notes: _____
_____
_____

Current value: $30   2008 est. value: $295

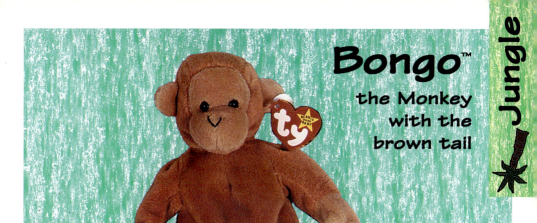

Bongo™

the Monkey
with the
brown tail

Birthday: _____August 17, 1995_____

Introduced: _____February 6, 1996_____

Retired Day: _____June 29, 1996_____

Date I Got It: _____

Where I Got It: _____

I Paid: $ _____ or

Who Gave It to Me: _____

Hang Tag Version: ☐   Tush Tag Version: ☐

Notes: _____

_____

_____

Current value: $85   2008 est. value: $375

Bongo™

the Monkey
with the
tan tail
(formerly
Nana)

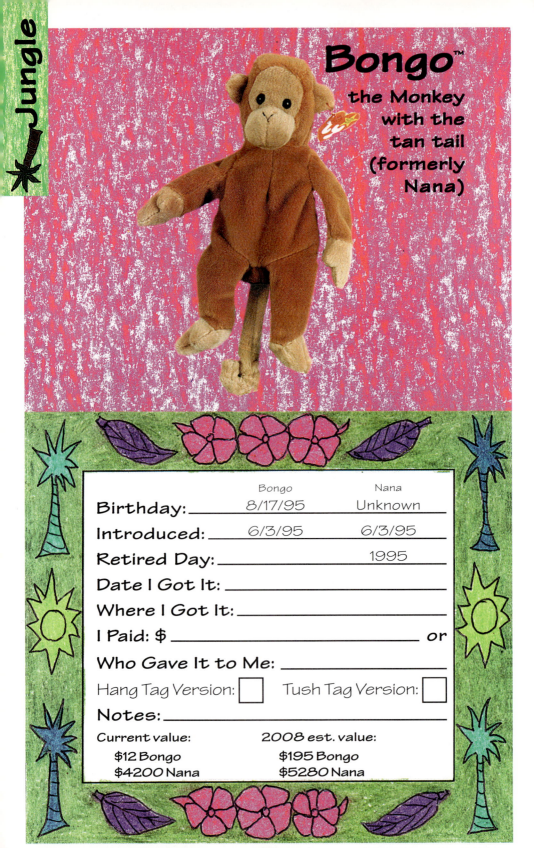

	Bongo	Nana
Birthday:	8/17/95	Unknown
Introduced:	6/3/95	6/3/95
Retired Day:		1995

Date I Got It: _____

Where I Got It: _____

I Paid: $ _____ or

Who Gave It to Me: _____

Hang Tag Version: ☐   Tush Tag Version: ☐

Notes: _____

Current value:
  $12 Bongo
  $4200 Nana

2008 est. value:
  $195 Bongo
  $5280 Nana

Congo™
the Gorilla

Birthday: November 9, 1996

Introduced: June 15, 1996

Retired Day: _____

Date I Got It: _____

Where I Got It: _____

I Paid: $ _____ or

Who Gave It to Me: _____

Hang Tag Version: ☐   Tush Tag Version: ☐

Notes: _____
_____
_____

Current value: $12   2008 est. value: $195

Freckles™
the Leopard

Birthday: June 3, 1996

Introduced: June 15, 1996

Retired Day: _____

Date I Got It: _____

Where I Got It: _____

I Paid: $ _____ **or**

Who Gave It to Me: _____

Hang Tag Version: ☐   Tush Tag Version: ☐

Notes: _____
_____
_____

Current value: $12   2008 est. value: $185

Happy™
the Hippo
Gray &
Lavender

	Gray	Lavender
Birthday:	2/25/94	2/25/94
Introduced:	6/25/94	6/3/95
Retired Day:	6/3/95	5/1/98

Date I Got It: _____

Where I Got It: _____

I Paid: $ _____ or

Who Gave It to Me: _____

Hang Tag Version: ☐   Tush Tag Version: ☐

Notes: _____

Current value:
   $825 gray
   $25 lavender

2008 est. value:
   $1625 gray
   $325 lavender

Humphrey™
the Camel

* **Not really the jungle, but close!**

Birthday: Unknown

Introduced: June 25, 1994

Retired Day: June 15, 1995

Date I Got It: _____

Where I Got It: _____

I Paid: $ _____ **or**

Who Gave It to Me: _____

Hang Tag Version: ☐   Tush Tag Version: ☐

Notes: _____
_____
_____

Current value: $2200   2008 est. value: $4250

Mel™

the Koala

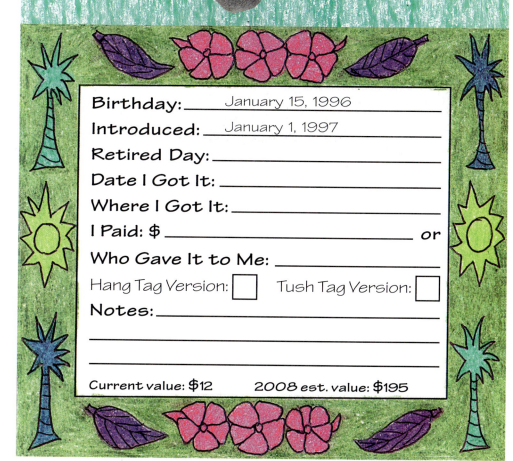

Birthday: _January 15, 1996_

Introduced: _January 1, 1997_

Retired Day: _____

Date I Got It: _____

Where I Got It: _____

I Paid: $ _____ **or**

Who Gave It to Me: _____

Hang Tag Version: ☐   Tush Tag Version: ☐

Notes: _____

_____

_____

Current value: $12   2008 est. value: $195

65

Peanut™

the Elephant
Royal Blue &
Light Blue

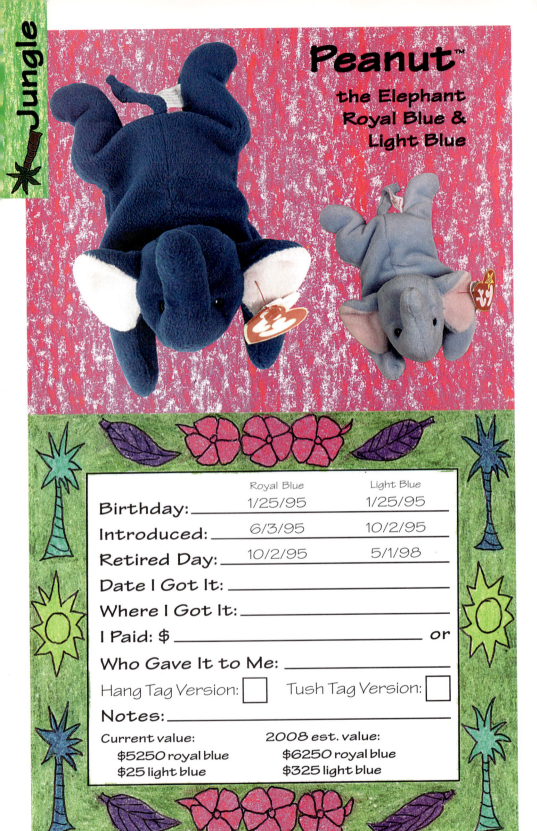

	Royal Blue	Light Blue
Birthday:	1/25/95	1/25/95
Introduced:	6/3/95	10/2/95
Retired Day:	10/2/95	5/1/98

Date I Got It: _____

Where I Got It: _____

I Paid: $ _____ or

Who Gave It to Me: _____

Hang Tag Version: ☐   Tush Tag Version: ☐

Notes: _____

Current value:
   $5250 royal blue
   $25 light blue

2008 est. value:
   $6250 royal blue
   $325 light blue

Pouch™
the Kangaroo

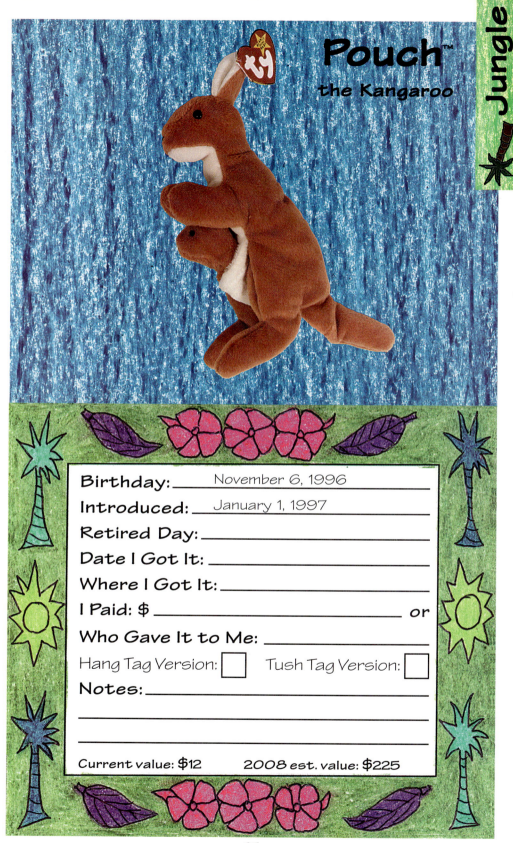

Birthday: _November 6, 1996_

Introduced: _January 1, 1997_

Retired Day: _____

Date I Got It: _____

Where I Got It: _____

I Paid: $ _____ or

Who Gave It to Me: _____

Hang Tag Version: ☐   Tush Tag Version: ☐

Notes: _____
_____
_____

Current value: $12   2008 est. value: $225

67

Roary™
the Lion

Birthday: _February 20, 1996_

Introduced: _May 11, 1997_

Retired Day: _____

Date I Got It: _____

Where I Got It: _____

I Paid: $ _____ **or**

Who Gave It to Me: _____

Hang Tag Version: ☐   Tush Tag Version: ☐

Notes: _____
_____
_____

Current value: **$12**   2008 est. value: **$225**

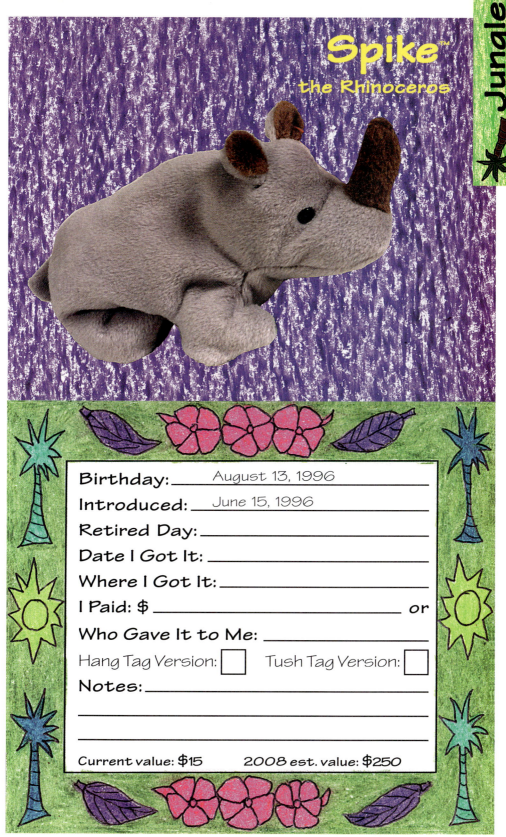

Spike™
the Rhinoceros

Birthday: _____August 13, 1996_____

Introduced: _____June 15, 1996_____

Retired Day: _____

Date I Got It: _____

Where I Got It: _____

I Paid: $ _____ or

Who Gave It to Me: _____

Hang Tag Version: ☐   Tush Tag Version: ☐

Notes: _____

_____

_____

Current value: $15   2008 est. value: $250

69

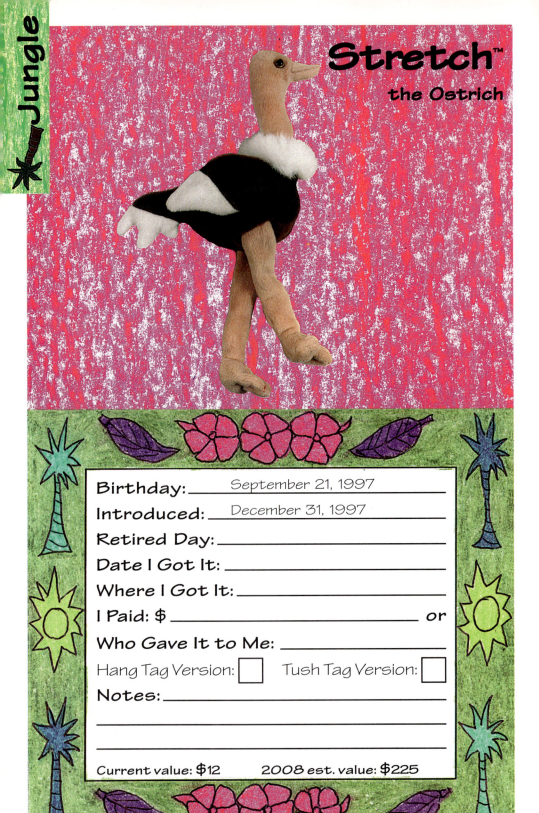

Jungle

Stretch™

the Ostrich

Birthday: _September 21, 1997_

Introduced: _December 31, 1997_

Retired Day: _____

Date I Got It: _____

Where I Got It: _____

I Paid: $ _____ or

Who Gave It to Me: _____

Hang Tag Version: ☐   Tush Tag Version: ☐

Notes: _____
_____
_____

Current value: $12   2008 est. value: $225

Stripes™

the Tiger
with thin
stripes &
wide stripes

Jungle

	thin stripes	wide stripes
Birthday:	6/11/95	6/11/95
Introduced:	1/7/96	6/3/96
Retired Day:	6/3/96	5/1/98

Date I Got It: _____

Where I Got It: _____

I Paid: $ _____ **or**

Who Gave It to Me: _____

Hang Tag Version: ☐   **Tush Tag Version:** ☐

Notes: _____

Current value:
  $325 thin stripes
  $25 wide stripes

2008 est. value:
  $950 thin stripes
  $325 wide stripes

Twigs™
the Giraffe

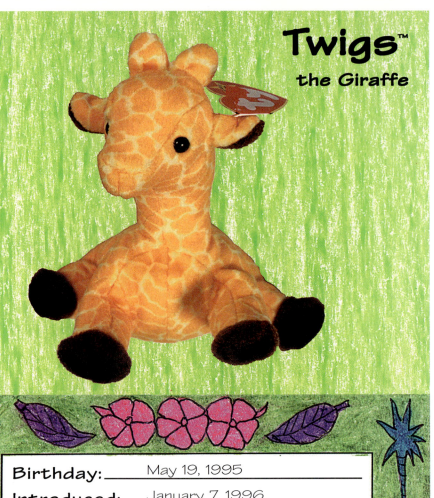

Birthday: _May 19, 1995_

Introduced: _January 7, 1996_

Retired Day: _May 1, 1998_

Date I Got It: _____

Where I Got It: _____

I Paid: $ _____ **or**

Who Gave It to Me: _____

Hang Tag Version: ☐   Tush Tag Version: ☐

Notes: _____
_____
_____

Current value: $25   2008 est. value: $295

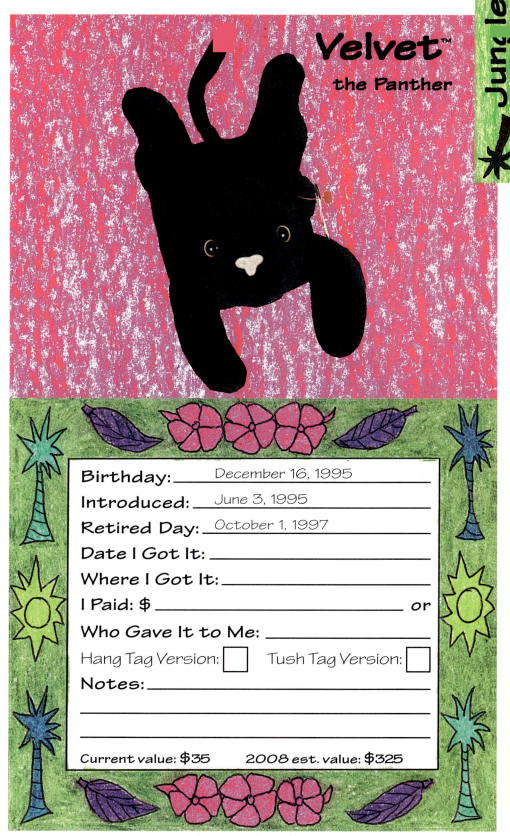

Velvet™
the Panther

Birthday: _December 16, 1995_

Introduced: _June 3, 1995_

Retired Day: _October 1, 1997_

Date I Got It: _____

Where I Got It: _____

I Paid: $ _____ **or**

Who Gave It to Me: _____

Hang Tag Version: ☐   Tush Tag Version: ☐

Notes: _____

_____

_____

Current value: **$35**   2008 est. value: **$325**

Ziggy™
the Zebra

Birthday: _December 24, 1995_

Introduced: _June 3, 1995_

Retired Day: _May 1, 1998_

Date I Got It: _____

Where I Got It: _____

I Paid: $ _____ or

Who Gave It to Me: _____

Hang Tag Version: ☐   Tush Tag Version: ☐

Notes: _____
_____
_____

Current value: $30   2008 est. value: $325

Bucky™
the Beaver

Birthday: _June 8, 1995_

Introduced: _January 7, 1996_

Retired Day: _December 31, 1997_

Date I Got It: _____

Where I Got It: _____

I Paid: $ _____ **or**

Who Gave It to Me: _____

Hang Tag Version: ☐   Tush Tag Version: ☐

Notes: _____

_____

_____

Current value: **$45**   2008 est. value: **$350**

Chocolate™
the Moose

Birthday: April 27, 1993

Introduced: January 8, 1994

Retired Day: _____

Date I Got It: _____

Where I Got It: _____

I Paid: $ _____ or

Who Gave It to Me: _____

Hang Tag Version: ☐   Tush Tag Version: ☐

Notes: _____
_____
_____

Current value: $12   2008 est. value: $185

Ears™
the Brown Rabbit

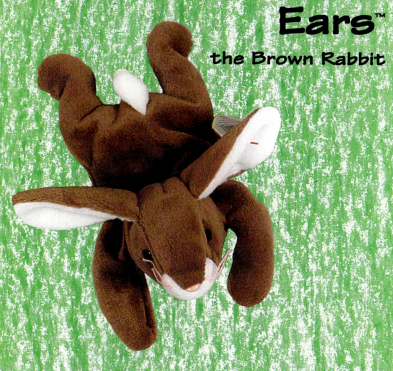

Birthday: _April 18, 1995_

Introduced: _January 7, 1996_

Retired Day: _May 1, 1998_

Date I Got It: _____

Where I Got It: _____

I Paid: $ _____ or

Who Gave It to Me: _____

Hang Tag Version: ☐   Tush Tag Version: ☐

Notes: _____
_____
_____

Current value: **$18**   2008 est. value: **$225**

77

Floppity™

the Lilac Bunny

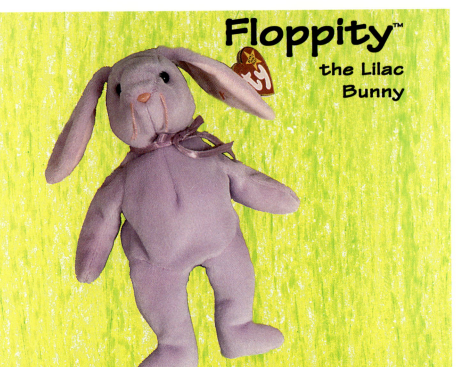

Birthday: _May 28, 1996_

Introduced: _January 1, 1997_

Retired Day: _May 1, 1998_

Date I Got It: _____

Where I Got It: _____

I Paid: $ _____ or

Who Gave It to Me: _____

Hang Tag Version: ☐   Tush Tag Version: ☐

Notes: _____

_____

_____

Current value: $25   2008 est. value: $275

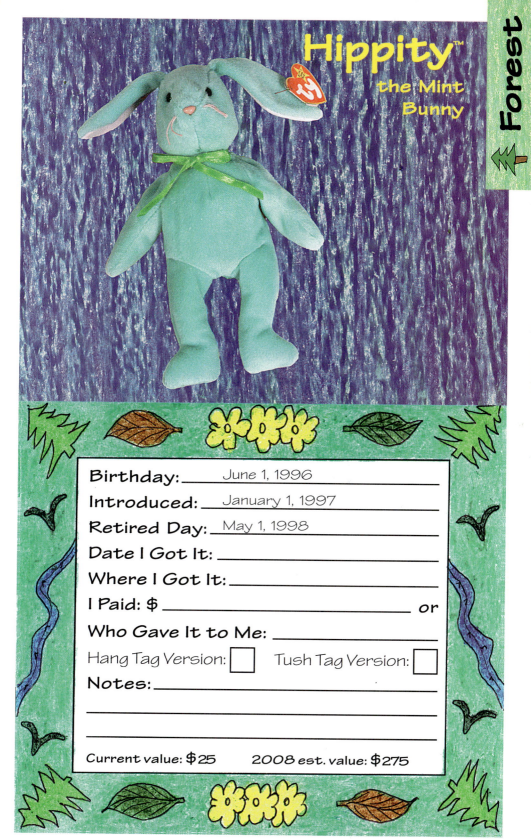

Hippity™
the Mint Bunny

Birthday: June 1, 1996

Introduced: January 1, 1997

Retired Day: May 1, 1998

Date I Got It: _____

Where I Got It: _____

I Paid: $ _____ **or**

Who Gave It to Me: _____

Hang Tag Version: ☐   Tush Tag Version: ☐

Notes: _____
_____
_____

Current value: $25   2008 est. value: $275

Hoppity™
the Rose Bunny

Birthday: _April 3, 1996_

Introduced: _January 1, 1997_

Retired Day: _May 1, 1998_

Date I Got It: _____

Where I Got It: _____

I Paid: $ _____ **or**

Who Gave It to Me: _____

Hang Tag Version: ☐   Tush Tag Version: ☐

Notes: _____
_____
_____

Current value: $25   2008 est. value: $275

Legs™
the Frog

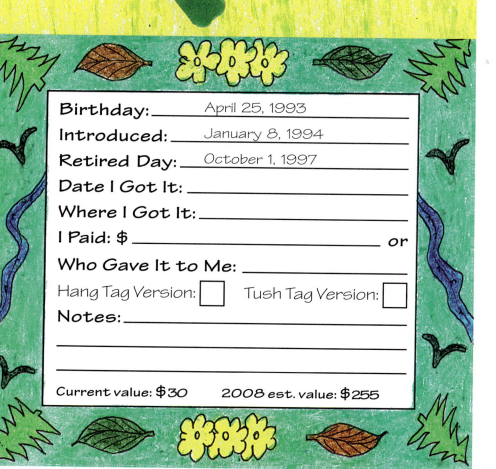

Birthday: April 25, 1993

Introduced: January 8, 1994

Retired Day: October 1, 1997

Date I Got It: _____

Where I Got It: _____

I Paid: $ _____ or

Who Gave It to Me: _____

Hang Tag Version: ☐   Tush Tag Version: ☐

Notes: _____

_____

_____

Current value: $30   2008 est. value: $255

Nuts™
the Squirrel

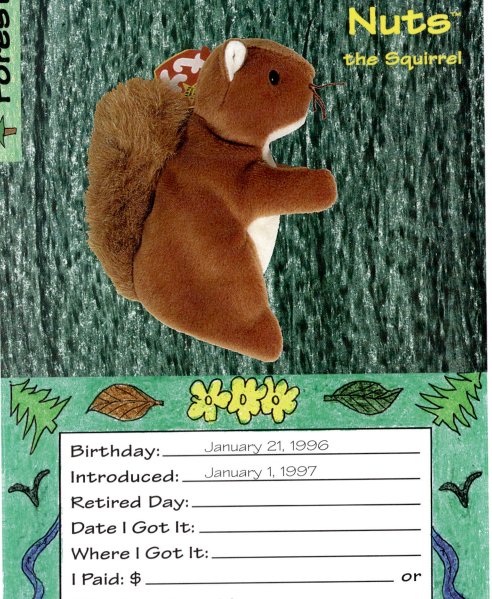

Birthday: _January 21, 1996_

Introduced: _January 1, 1997_

Retired Day: _____

Date I Got It: _____

Where I Got It: _____

I Paid: $ _____ or

Who Gave It to Me: _____

Hang Tag Version: ☐   Tush Tag Version: ☐

Notes: _____
_____
_____

Current value: **$12**   2008 est. value: **$165**

Ringo™
the Raccoon

Birthday: _July 14, 1995_

Introduced: _January 7, 1996_

Retired Day: _____

Date I Got It: _____

Where I Got It: _____

I Paid: $ _____ **or**

Who Gave It to Me: _____

Hang Tag Version: ☐   Tush Tag Version: ☐

Notes: _____

_____

_____

Current value: **$12**   2008 est. value: **$165**

Sly™
the Brown Bellied & White Bellied Fox

	Brown Bellied	White Bellied
Birthday:	9/12/96	9/12/96
Introduced:	6/15/96	8/6/96

Retired Day: 8/6/96

Date I Got It: _____

Where I Got It: _____

I Paid: $ _____ or

Who Gave It to Me: _____

Hang Tag Version: ☐   Tush Tag Version: ☐

Notes: _____

Current value:
$195 brown
$12 white

2008 est. value:
$575 brown
$175 white

Smoochy™
the Frog

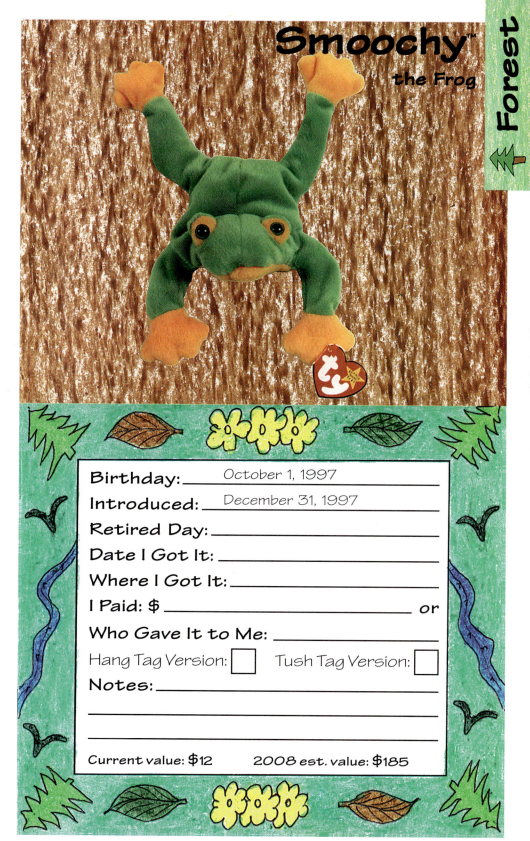

Birthday: _October 1, 1997_

Introduced: _December 31, 1997_

Retired Day: _____

Date I Got It: _____

Where I Got It: _____

I Paid: $ _____ or

Who Gave It to Me: _____

Hang Tag Version: ☐   Tush Tag Version: ☐

Notes: _____

_____

_____

Current value: $12   2008 est. value: $185

Stinky™
the Skunk

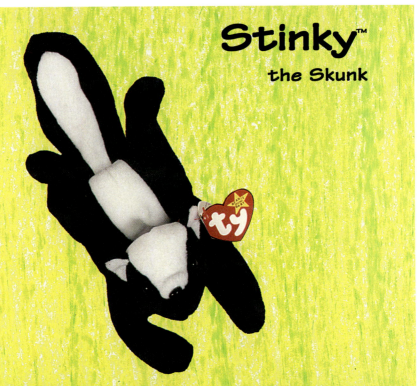

Birthday: February 13, 1995

Introduced: June 3, 1995

Retired Day: _____

Date I Got It: _____

Where I Got It: _____

I Paid: $ _____ **or**

Who Gave It to Me: _____

Hang Tag Version: ☐   Tush Tag Version: ☐

Notes: _____
_____
_____

Current value: $12   2008 est. value: $150

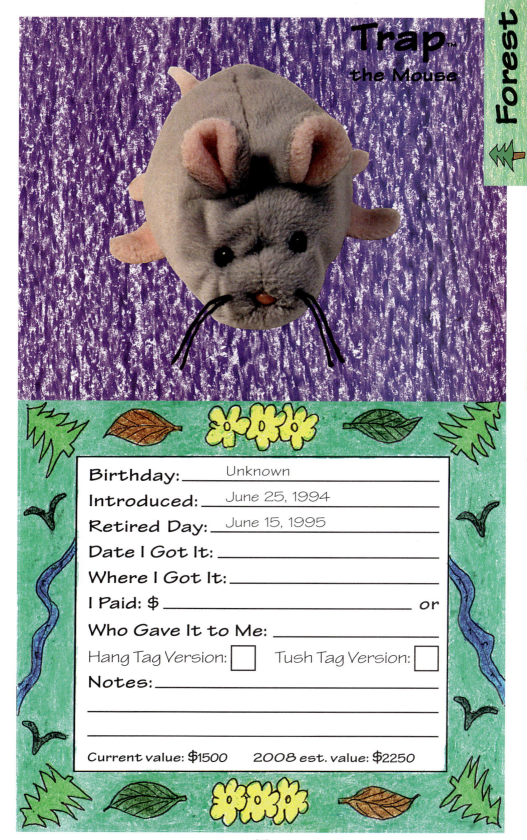

Trap™
the Mouse

Birthday: _____ Unknown _____

Introduced: ____ June 25, 1994 _____

Retired Day: ___ June 15, 1995 _____

Date I Got It: _____

Where I Got It: _____

I Paid: $ _____ **or**

Who Gave It to Me: _____

Hang Tag Version: ☐   Tush Tag Version: ☐

Notes: _____

_____

_____

Current value: $1500   2008 est. value: $2250

87

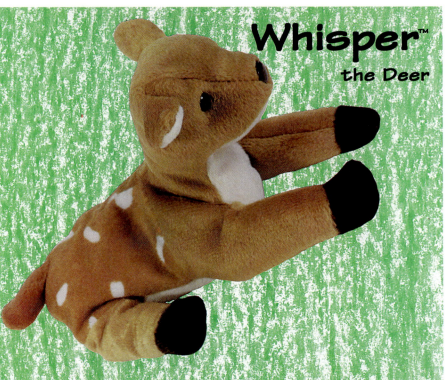

Forest

Whisper™
the Deer

Birthday: _____April 5, 1997_____

Introduced: _____May 30, 1998_____

Retired Day: _____

Date I Got It: _____

Where I Got It: _____

I Paid: $ _____ or

Who Gave It to Me: _____

Hang Tag Version: ☐   Tush Tag Version: ☐

Notes: _____

_____

_____

Current value: $15   2008 est. value: $325

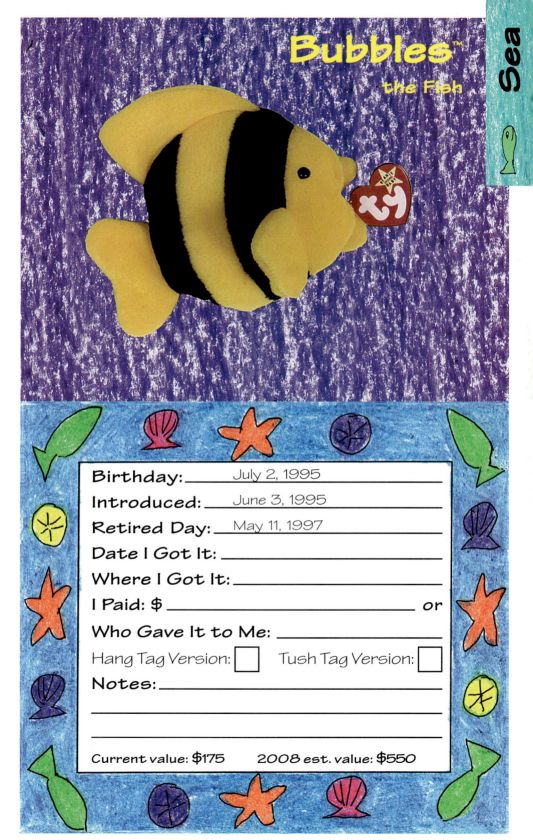

Bubbles™
the Fish

Sea

Birthday: _____July 2, 1995_____

Introduced: _____June 3, 1995_____

Retired Day: _____May 11, 1997_____

Date I Got It: _____

Where I Got It: _____

I Paid: $ _____ **or**

Who Gave It to Me: _____

Hang Tag Version: ☐   Tush Tag Version: ☐

Notes: _____

_____

_____

Current value: $175   2008 est. value: $550

Claude™
the Crab

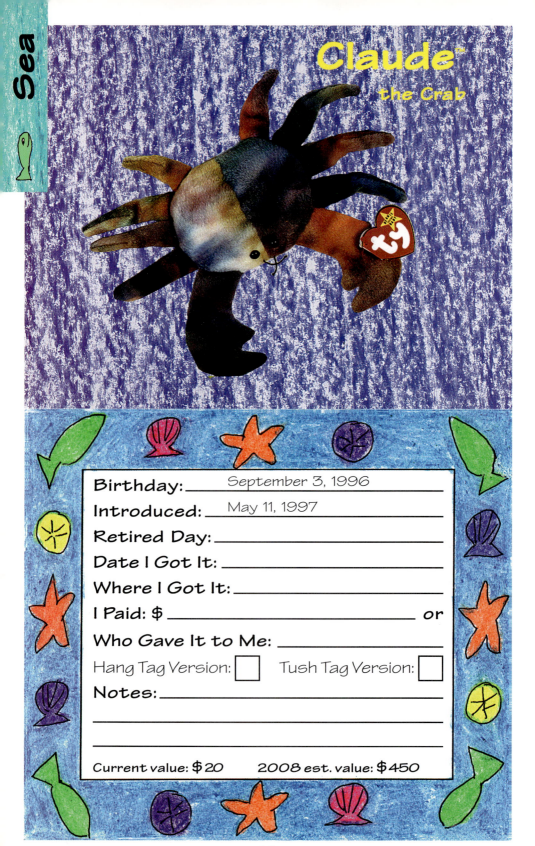

Birthday: _September 3, 1996_

Introduced: _May 11, 1997_

Retired Day: _____

Date I Got It: _____

Where I Got It: _____

I Paid: $ _____ or

Who Gave It to Me: _____

Hang Tag Version: ☐   Tush Tag Version: ☐

Notes: _____
_____
_____

Current value: $20   2008 est. value: $450

Coral™

the Fish

Birthday: _March 2, 1995_

Introduced: _June 3, 1995_

Retired Day: _January 1, 1997_

Date I Got It: _____

Where I Got It: _____

I Paid: $ _____ **or**

Who Gave It to Me: _____

Hang Tag Version: ☐   Tush Tag Version: ☐

Notes: _____
_____
_____

Current value: **$225**   2008 est. value: **$675**

Crunch™

the Shark

Birthday: _January 13, 1996_

Introduced: _January 1, 1997_

Retired Day: _____

Date I Got It: _____

Where I Got It: _____

I Paid: $ _____ or

Who Gave It to Me: _____

Hang Tag Version: ☐   Tush Tag Version: ☐

Notes: _____

_____

_____

Current value: $15   2008 est. value: $225

Digger™
the Crab
Orange & Red

	orange	red
Birthday:	8/23/95	8/23/95
Introduced:	6/25/94	6/3/95
Retired Day:	6/3/95	5/11/97

Date I Got It: _____

Where I Got It: _____

I Paid: $ _____ or

Who Gave It to Me: _____

Hang Tag Version: ☐   Tush Tag Version: ☐

Notes: _____

Current value:	2008 est. value:
$950 orange	$1650 orange
$125 red	$425 red

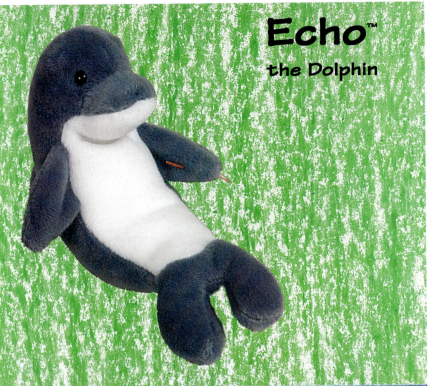

Echo™
the Dolphin

Birthday: December 21, 1996

Introduced: May 11, 1997

Retired Day: May 1, 1998

Date I Got It: _____

Where I Got It: _____

I Paid: $ _____ **or**

Who Gave It to Me: _____

Hang Tag Version: ☐   Tush Tag Version: ☐

Notes: _____

_____

_____

Current value: $25   2008 est. value: $275

Flash™
the Dolphin

Birthday: May 13, 1993

Introduced: January 8, 1994

Retired Day: May 11, 1997

Date I Got It: _____

Where I Got It: _____

I Paid: $ _____ or

Who Gave It to Me: _____

Hang Tag Version: ☐   Tush Tag Version: ☐

Notes: _____
_____
_____

Current value: $145   2008 est. value: $475

Goldie™
the Goldfish

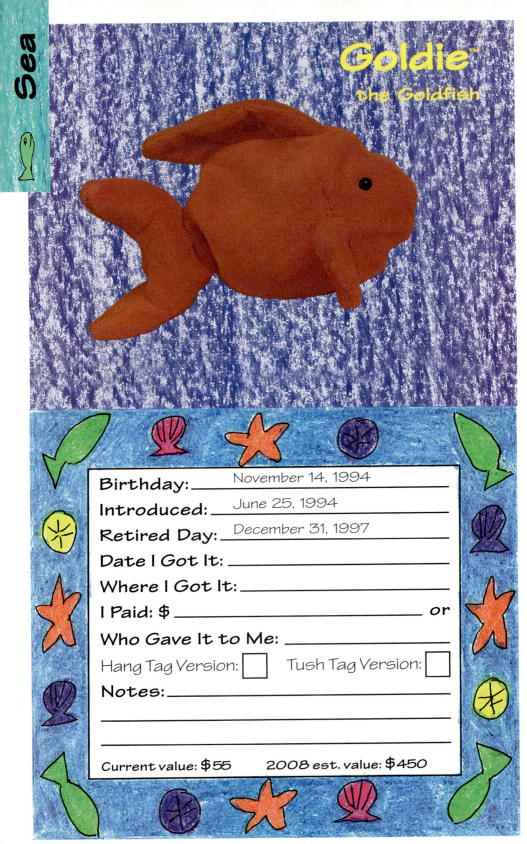

Birthday: November 14, 1994

Introduced: June 25, 1994

Retired Day: December 31, 1997

Date I Got It: _____

Where I Got It: _____

I Paid: $ _____ **or**

Who Gave It to Me: _____

Hang Tag Version: ☐   Tush Tag Version: ☐

Notes: _____
_____
_____

Current value: $55   2008 est. value: $450

Inky™
the Pink Octopus

Birthday: _November 29, 1994_

Introduced: _June 3, 1995_

Retired Day: _May 1, 1998_

Date I Got It: _____

Where I Got It: _____

I Paid: $ _____ or

Who Gave It to Me: _____

Hang Tag Version: ☐   Tush Tag Version: ☐

Notes: _____

_____

_____

Current value: **$50**   2008 est. value: **$475**

Inky™

the Tan Octopus
without a mouth
& with a mouth

	without mouth	with mouth
Birthday:	11/29/94	11/29/94
Introduced:	6/25/94	9/12/94
Retired Day:	9/12/94	5/1/98

Date I Got It: _____

Where I Got It: _____

I Paid: $ _____ or

Who Gave It to Me: _____

Hang Tag Version: ☐   Tush Tag Version: ☐

Notes: _____

Current value:
$795 w/o mouth
$695 w/ mouth

2008 est. value:
$1495 w/o mouth
$1455 w/ mouth

Jolly™
the Walrus

Birthday: _December 2, 1996_

Introduced: _May 11, 1997_

Retired Day: _May 1, 1998_

Date I Got It: _____

Where I Got It: _____

I Paid: $ _____ or

Who Gave It to Me: _____

Hang Tag Version: ☐   Tush Tag Version: ☐

Notes: _____
_____
_____

Current value: $30   2008 est. value: $295

Manny™
the Manatee

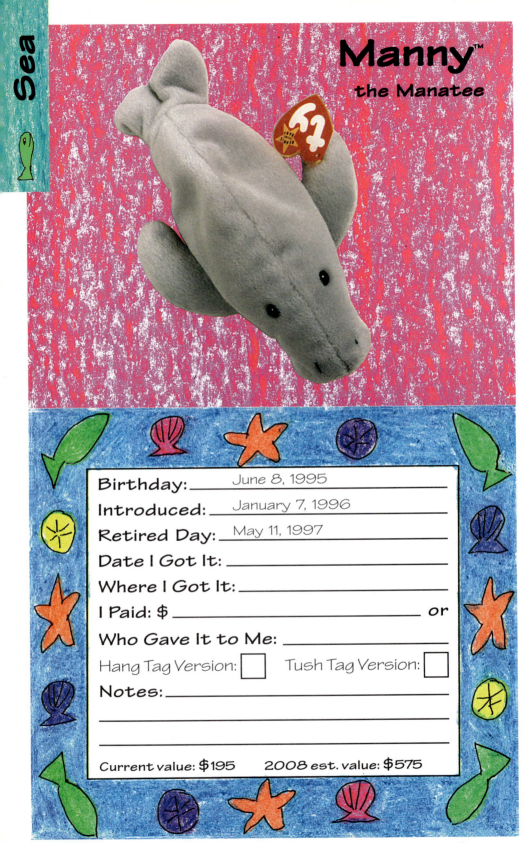

Birthday: June 8, 1995

Introduced: January 7, 1996

Retired Day: May 11, 1997

Date I Got It: _____

Where I Got It: _____

I Paid: $ _____ **or**

Who Gave It to Me: _____

Hang Tag Version: ☐   Tush Tag Version: ☐

Notes: _____
_____
_____

Current value: $195   2008 est. value: $575

Patti˜
the Maroon & Magenta Platypus

	maroon	magenta
Birthday:	1/6/93	1/6/93
Introduced:	1/8/94	2/28/95
Retired Day:	2/28/95	5/1/98

Date I Got It: _____

Where I Got It: _____

I Paid: $ _____ or

Who Gave It to Me: _____

Hang Tag Version: ☐   Tush Tag Version: ☐

Notes: _____

Current value:
   $1000 maroon
   $28 magenta

2008 est. value:
   $1495 maroon
   $325 magenta

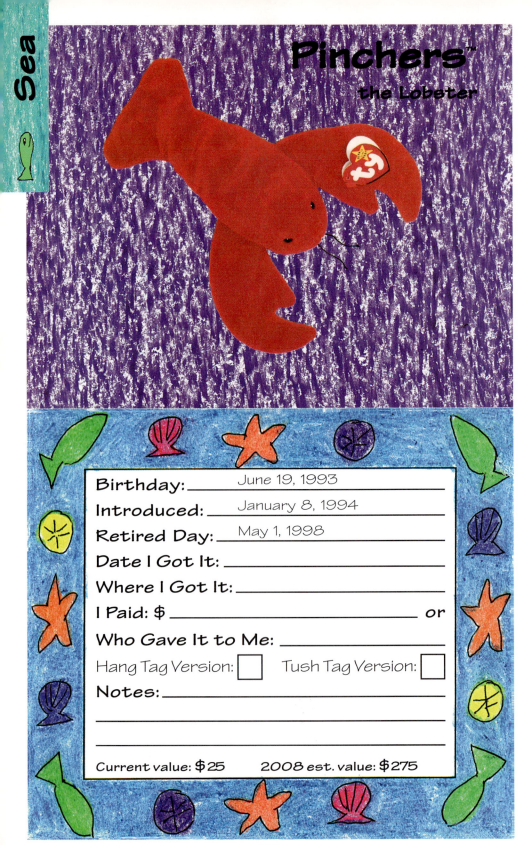

Pinchers™
the Lobster

Birthday: June 19, 1993

Introduced: January 8, 1994

Retired Day: May 1, 1998

Date I Got It: _____

Where I Got It: _____

I Paid: $ _____ **or**

Who Gave It to Me: _____

Hang Tag Version: ☐   Tush Tag Version: ☐

Notes: _____
_____
_____

Current value: $25   2008 est. value: $275

Seamore™
the Seal

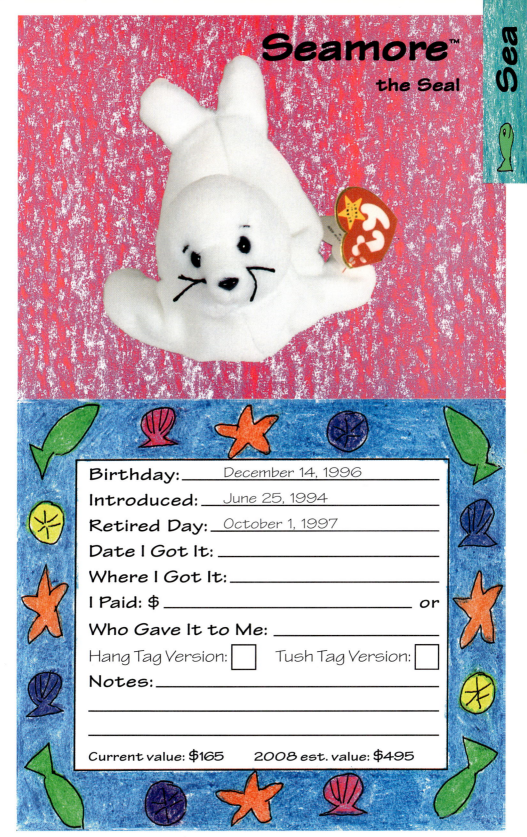

Birthday: _December 14, 1996_

Introduced: _June 25, 1994_

Retired Day: _October 1, 1997_

Date I Got It: _____

Where I Got It: _____

I Paid: $ _____ or

Who Gave It to Me: _____

Hang Tag Version: ☐   Tush Tag Version: ☐

Notes: _____
_____
_____

Current value: $165   2008 est. value: $495

Seaweed™
the Otter

Birthday: March 19, 1996

Introduced: January 7, 1996

Retired Day: _____

Date I Got It: _____

Where I Got It: _____

I Paid: $ _____ or

Who Gave It to Me: _____

Hang Tag Version: ☐   Tush Tag Version: ☐

Notes: _____

_____

_____

Current value: $20   2008 est. value: $275

Splash™
the Orca Whale

Birthday: _July 8, 1993_

Introduced: _January 8, 1994_

Retired Day: _May 11, 1997_

Date I Got It: _____

Where I Got It: _____

I Paid: $ _____ **or**

Who Gave It to Me: _____

Hang Tag Version: ☐   Tush Tag Version: ☐

Notes: _____
_____
_____

Current value: $135   2008 est. value: $375

Sting™
the Ray

Birthday: August 27, 1995

Introduced: June 3, 1995

Retired Day: January 1, 1997

Date I Got It: _____

Where I Got It: _____

I Paid: $ _____ or

Who Gave It to Me: _____

Hang Tag Version: ☐   **Tush Tag Version:** ☐

Notes: _____
_____
_____

Current value: $225   2008 est. value: $650

Tusk™
the Walrus

Sea

Birthday: September 18, 1995

Introduced: January 7, 1995

Retired Day: January 1, 1997

Date I Got It: _____

Where I Got It: _____

I Paid: $ _____ or

Who Gave It to Me: _____

Hang Tag Version: ☐   Tush Tag Version: ☐

Notes: _____
_____
_____

Current value: $175   2008 est. value: $525

Waddle™
the Penguin

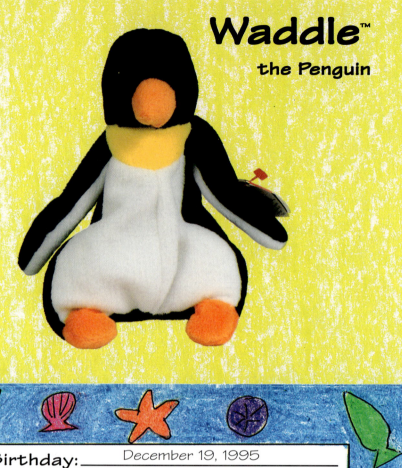

Birthday: _December 19, 1995_

Introduced: _June 3, 1995_

Retired Day: _May 1, 1998_

Date I Got It: _____

Where I Got It: _____

I Paid: $ _____ or

Who Gave It to Me: _____

Hang Tag Version: ☐   Tush Tag Version: ☐

Notes: _____

_____

_____

Current value: $28   2008 est. value: $275

Waves™
the Whale

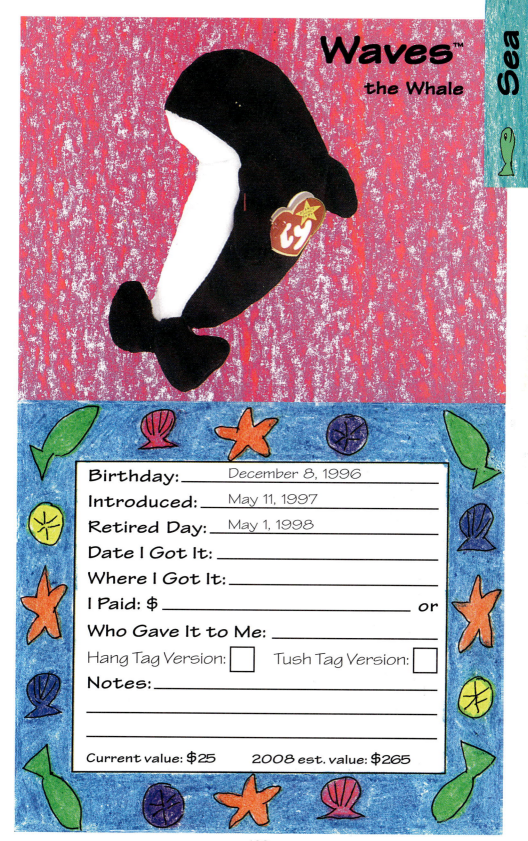

Birthday:	December 8, 1996
Introduced:	May 11, 1997
Retired Day:	May 1, 1998
Date I Got It:	
Where I Got It:	
I Paid: $	_____ or
Who Gave It to Me:	

Hang Tag Version: ☐   Tush Tag Version: ☐

Notes: _____

Current value: $25   2008 est. value: $265

Ally™
the Alligator

Birthday: _____ March 14, 1994 _____

Introduced: _____ June 25, 1994 _____

Retired Day: _____ October 1, 1997 _____

Date I Got It: _____

Where I Got It: _____

I Paid: $ _____ or

Who Gave It to Me: _____

Hang Tag Version: ☐   Tush Tag Version: ☐

Notes: _____

_____

_____

Current value: $65   2008 est. value: $475

Hissy™
the Snake

Crawlers

Birthday: _April 4, 1997_

Introduced: _December 31, 1997_

Retired Day: _____

Date I Got It: _____

Where I Got It: _____

I Paid: $ _____ **or**

Who Gave It to Me: _____

Hang Tag Version: ☐   Tush Tag Version: ☐

Notes: _____
_____
_____

Current value: **$15**   2008 est. value: **$350**

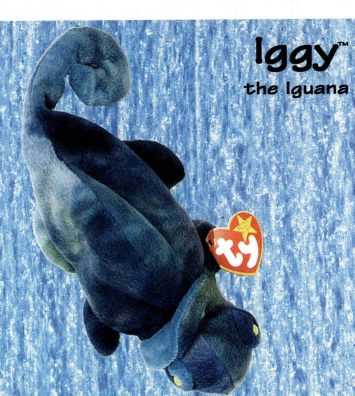

Iggy™
the Iguana

Birthday: _August 12, 1997_

Introduced: _December 31, 1997_

Retired Day: _____

Date I Got It: _____

Where I Got It: _____

I Paid: $ _____ **or**

Who Gave It to Me: _____

Hang Tag Version: ☐   Tush Tag Version: ☐

Notes: _____
_____
_____

Current value: **$12**   2008 est. value: **$275**

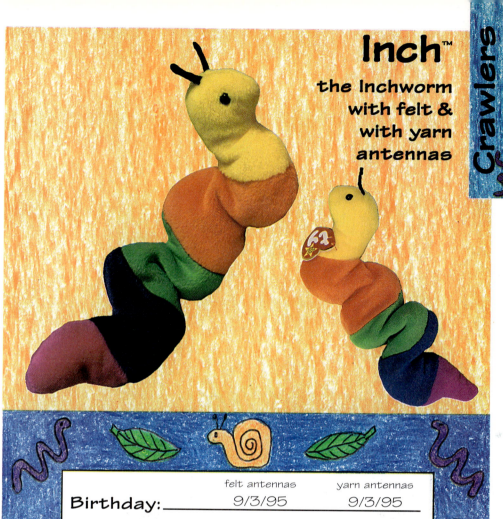

Inch™ the Inchworm with felt & with yarn antennas

Crawlers

	felt antennas	yarn antennas
Birthday:	9/3/95	9/3/95
Introduced:	6/3/95	1996
Retired Day:	1996	5/1/98

Date I Got It: _____

Where I Got It: _____

I Paid: $ _____ or

Who Gave It to Me: _____

Hang Tag Version: ☐   Tush Tag Version: ☐

Notes: _____

Current value:
  $195 felt antennas
  $25 yarn antennas

2008 est. value:
  $595 felt antennas
  $295 yarn antennas

Lizzy™

the Lizard
Tie-dyed &
Blue

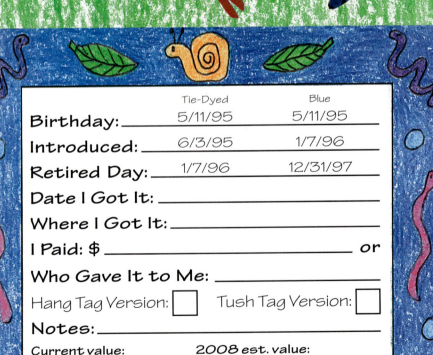

	Tie-Dyed	Blue
Birthday:	5/11/95	5/11/95
Introduced:	6/3/95	1/7/96
Retired Day:	1/7/96	12/31/97

Date I Got It: _____

Where I Got It: _____

I Paid: $ _____ or

Who Gave It to Me: _____

Hang Tag Version: ☐   Tush Tag Version: ☐

Notes: _____

Current value: 2008 est. value:

$1050 tie-dyed $2250 tie-dyed
$35 blue $335 blue

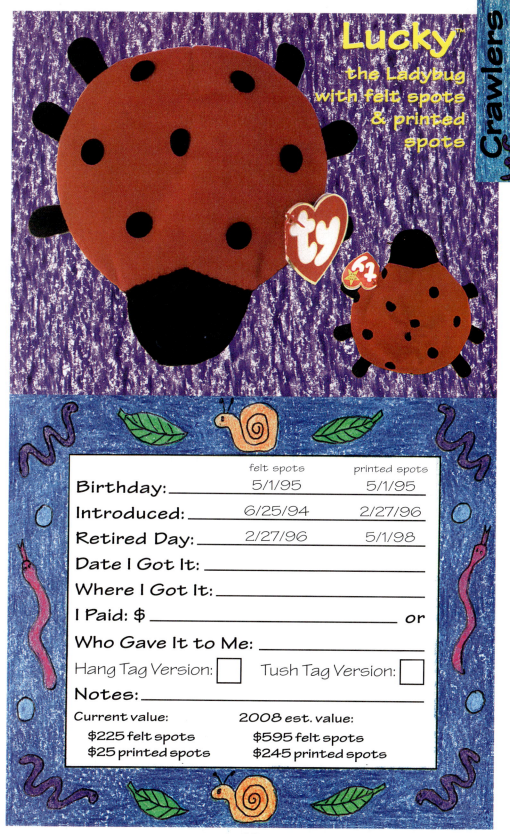

Lucky™
the Ladybug
with felt spots
& printed
spots

	felt spots	printed spots
Birthday:	5/1/95	5/1/95
Introduced:	6/25/94	2/27/96
Retired Day:	2/27/96	5/1/98

Date I Got It: _____

Where I Got It: _____

I Paid: $ _____ or

Who Gave It to Me: _____

Hang Tag Version: ☐   Tush Tag Version: ☐

Notes: _____

Current value: 2008 est. value:
  $225 felt spots $595 felt spots
  $25 printed spots $245 printed spots

Rainbow™

the Chameleon
without and
with tongue

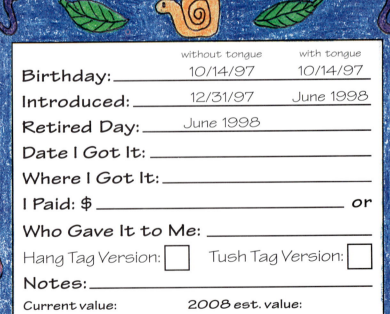

	without tongue	with tongue
Birthday:	10/14/97	10/14/97
Introduced:	12/31/97	June 1998
Retired Day:	June 1998	

Date I Got It: _____

Where I Got It: _____

I Paid: $ _____ **or**

Who Gave It to Me: _____

Hang Tag Version: ☐   **Tush Tag Version:** ☐

Notes: _____

Current value:
$25 without tongue
$15 with tongue

2008 est. value:
$325 without tongue
$275 with tongue

Slither™
the Snake

Birthday: _Unknown_

Introduced: _June 25, 1994_

Retired Day: _June 15, 1995_

Date I Got It: _____

Where I Got It: _____

I Paid: $ _____ or

Who Gave It to Me: _____

Hang Tag Version: ☐   Tush Tag Version: ☐

Notes: _____

_____

_____

Current value: $2250   2008 est. value: $3250

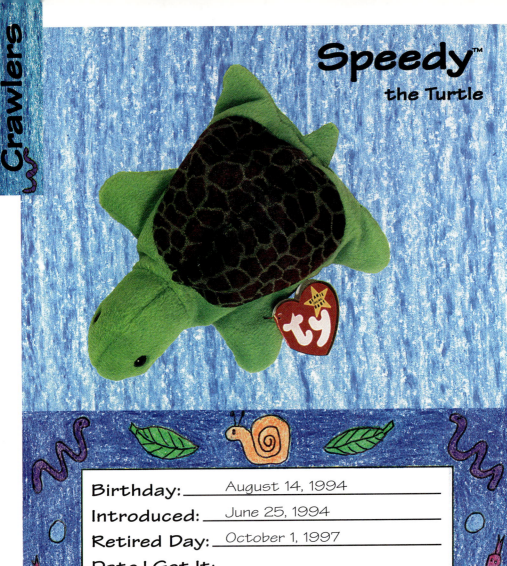

Speedy™
the Turtle

Birthday: _August 14, 1994_

Introduced: _June 25, 1994_

Retired Day: _October 1, 1997_

Date I Got It: _____

Where I Got It: _____

I Paid: $ _____ **or**

Who Gave It to Me: _____

Hang Tag Version: ☐   Tush Tag Version: ☐

Notes: _____
_____
_____

Current value: $40   2008 est. value: $325

Spinner™
the Spider

Birthday: _October 28, 1996_

Introduced: _October 1, 1997_

Retired Day: _____

Date I Got It: _____

Where I Got It: _____

I Paid: $ _____ **or**

Who Gave It to Me: _____

Hang Tag Version: ☐   Tush Tag Version: ☐

Notes: _____

_____

_____

Current value: $12   2008 est. value: $245

Stinger™
the Scorpion

Birthday: September 29, 1997

Introduced: May 30, 1998

Retired Day: _____

Date I Got It: _____

Where I Got It: _____

I Paid: $ _____ or

Who Gave It to Me: _____

Hang Tag Version: ☐   Tush Tag Version: ☐

Notes: _____

_____

_____

Current value: $12   2008 est. value: $225

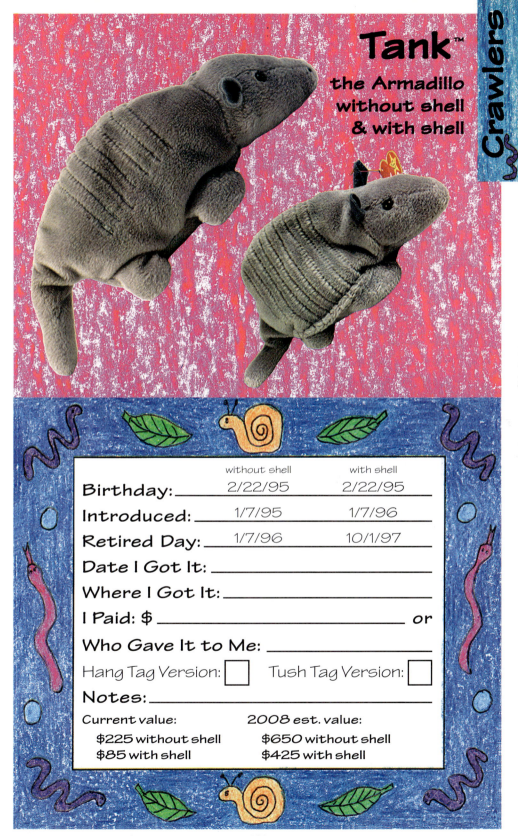

Tank™
the Armadillo
without shell
& with shell

	without shell	with shell
Birthday:	2/22/95	2/22/95
Introduced:	1/7/95	1/7/96
Retired Day:	1/7/96	10/1/97

Date I Got It: _____

Where I Got It: _____

I Paid: $ _____ **or**

Who Gave It to Me: _____

Hang Tag Version: ☐   Tush Tag Version: ☐

Notes: _____

Current value: 2008 est. value:
  $225 without shell $650 without shell
  $85 with shell $425 with shell

Web™
the Spider

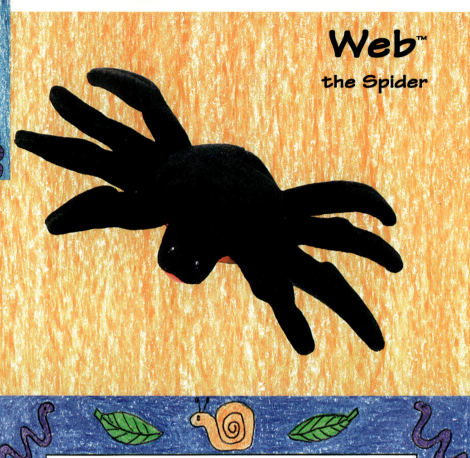

Birthday: _____Unknown_____

Introduced: _____June 25, 1994_____

Retired Day: _____January 7, 1996_____

Date I Got It: _____

Where I Got It: _____

I Paid: $ _____ or

Who Gave It to Me: _____

Hang Tag Version: ☐   Tush Tag Version: ☐

Notes: _____
_____
_____

Current value: $1500   2008 est. value: $2250

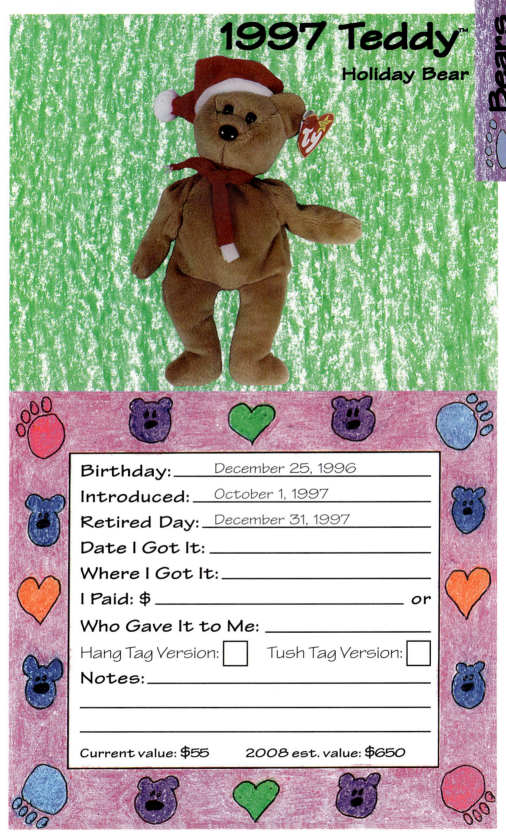

Birthday: _December 25, 1996_

Introduced: _October 1, 1997_

Retired Day: _December 31, 1997_

Date I Got It: _____

Where I Got It: _____

I Paid: $ _____ **or**

Who Gave It to Me: _____

Hang Tag Version: ☐   Tush Tag Version: ☐

Notes: _____

_____

_____

Current value: **$55**   2008 est. value: **$650**

Blackie™

the Black Bear

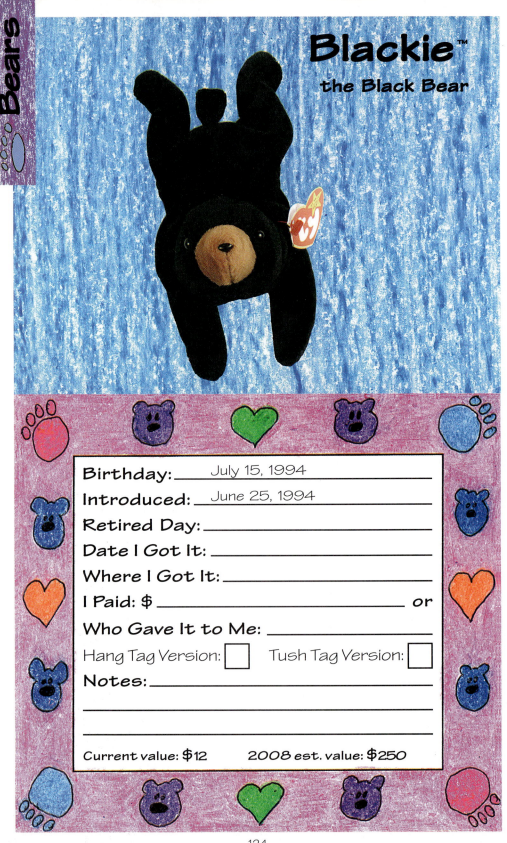

Birthday: July 15, 1994

Introduced: June 25, 1994

Retired Day: _____

Date I Got It: _____

Where I Got It: _____

I Paid: $ _____ **or**

Who Gave It to Me: _____

Hang Tag Version: ☐   Tush Tag Version: ☐

Notes: _____

_____

_____

Current value: $12   2008 est. value: $250

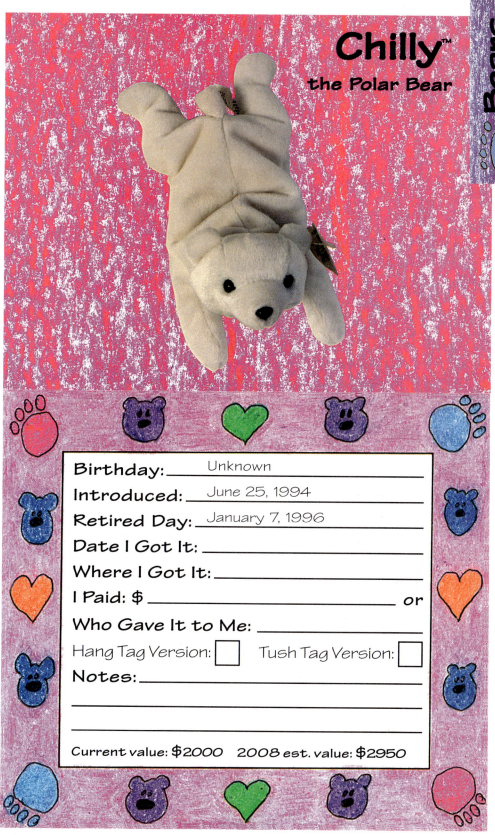

Chilly™
the Polar Bear

Bears

Birthday: Unknown

Introduced: June 25, 1994

Retired Day: January 7, 1996

Date I Got It: _____

Where I Got It: _____

I Paid: $ _____ or

Who Gave It to Me: _____

Hang Tag Version: ☐   Tush Tag Version: ☐

Notes: _____
_____
_____

Current value: $2000   2008 est. value: $2950

Clubby™
the B.B.O.C.™
exclusive Bear

Birthday: _Unknown_

Introduced: _May 1998_

Retired Day: _____

Date I Got It: _____

Where I Got It: _____

I Paid: $ _____ **or**

Who Gave It to Me: _____

Hang Tag Version: ☐   Tush Tag Version: ☐

Notes: _____
_____
_____

Current value: **$250**   2008 est. value: **$2250**

Cubbie™

the Brown Bear (formerly Brownie)

Bears

	Cubbie	Brownie
Birthday:	11/14/93	Unknown
Introduced:	1/8/94	1/8/94
Retired Day:	12/31/97	1994

Date I Got It: _____

Where I Got It: _____

I Paid: $ _____ or

Who Gave It to Me: _____

Hang Tag Version: ☐   Tush Tag Version: ☐

Notes: _____

Current value:
$35 Cubbie
$3850 Brownie

2008 est. value:
$375 Cubbie
$4750 Brownie

127

Curly™
the Brown Napped Bear

Birthday: April 12, 1996

Introduced: June 15, 1996

Retired Day: _____

Date I Got It: _____

Where I Got It: _____

I Paid: $ _____ **or**

Who Gave It to Me: _____

Hang Tag Version: ☐   Tush Tag Version: ☐

Notes: _____
_____
_____

Current value: $25   2008 est. value: $650

Erin™
the Bear

Bears

Birthday: March 17, 1997

Introduced: January 31, 1998

Retired Day: _____

Date I Got It: _____

Where I Got It: _____

I Paid: $ _____ or

Who Gave It to Me: _____

Hang Tag Version: ☐   Tush Tag Version: ☐

Notes: _____
_____
_____

Current value: $95   2008 est. value: $795

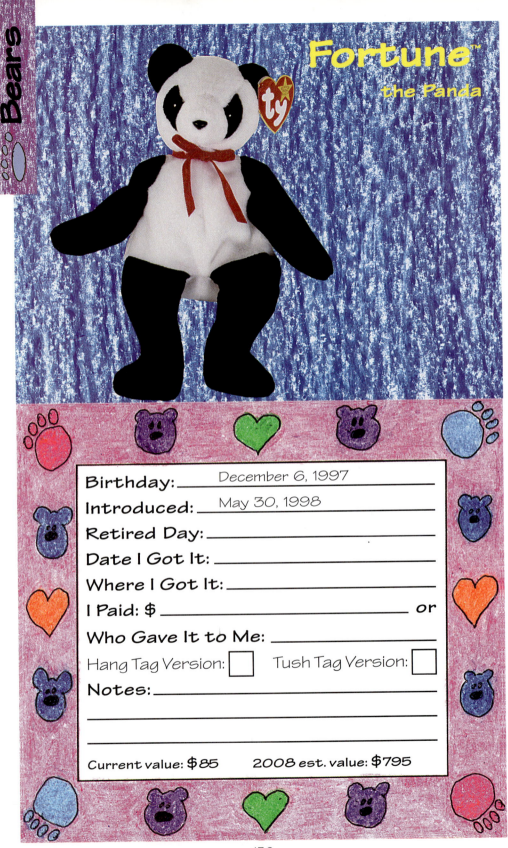

Fortune™
the Panda

Birthday: _December 6, 1997_

Introduced: _May 30, 1998_

Retired Day: _____

Date I Got It: _____

Where I Got It: _____

I Paid: $ _____ **or**

Who Gave It to Me: _____

Hang Tag Version: ☐   Tush Tag Version: ☐

Notes: _____
_____
_____

Current value: **$85**   2008 est. value: **$795**

Garcia™
the Bear

Bears

Birthday: August 1, 1995

Introduced: January 7, 1996

Retired Day: May 11, 1997

Date I Got It: _____

Where I Got It: _____

I Paid: $ _____ **or**

Who Gave It to Me: _____

Hang Tag Version: ☐   Tush Tag Version: ☐

Notes: _____

_____

_____

Current value: $195   2008 est. value: $1450

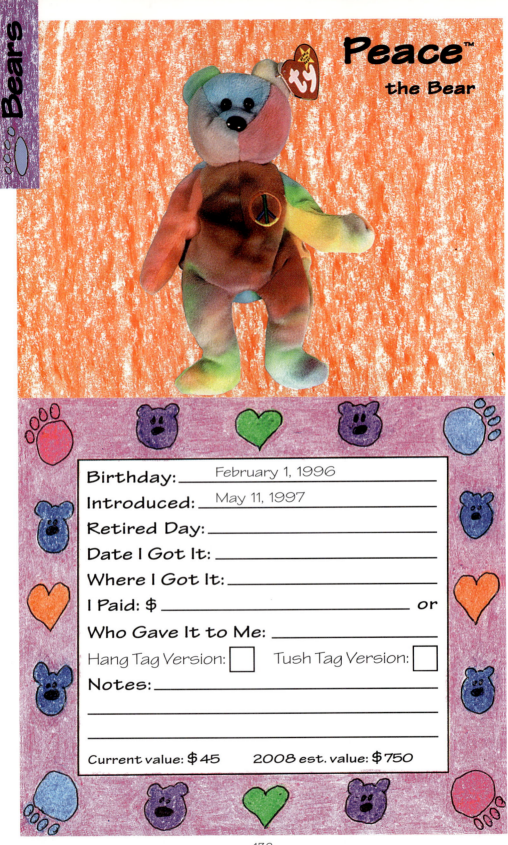

Peace™
the Bear

Birthday: February 1, 1996

Introduced: May 11, 1997

Retired Day: _____

Date I Got It: _____

Where I Got It: _____

I Paid: $ _____ **or**

Who Gave It to Me: _____

Hang Tag Version: ☐   Tush Tag Version: ☐

Notes: _____

_____

_____

Current value: **$45**   2008 est. value: **$750**

Peking™
the Panda

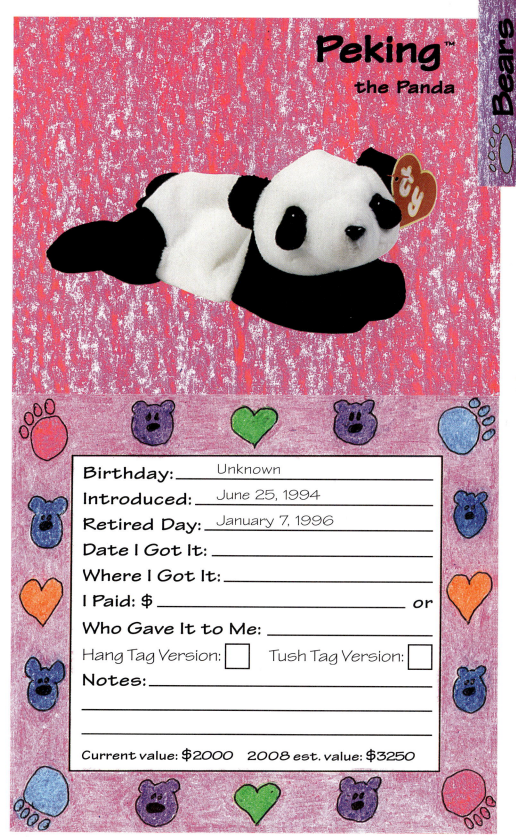

Birthday: _Unknown_

Introduced: _June 25, 1994_

Retired Day: _January 7, 1996_

Date I Got It: _____

Where I Got It: _____

I Paid: $ _____ **or**

Who Gave It to Me: _____

Hang Tag Version: ☐   Tush Tag Version: ☐

Notes: _____

_____

_____

Current value: $2000   2008 est. value: $3250

Princess™
the Bear

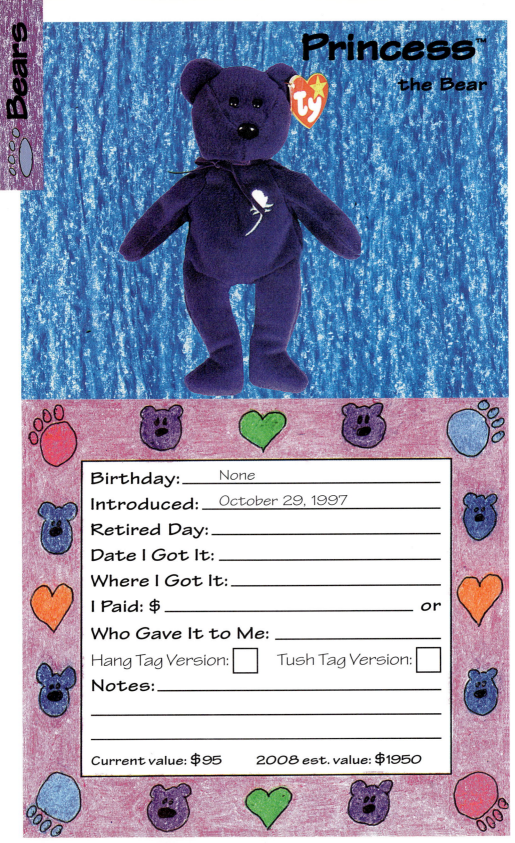

Birthday: _____ None _____

Introduced: _____ October 29, 1997 _____

Retired Day: _____

Date I Got It: _____

Where I Got It: _____

I Paid: $ _____ or

Who Gave It to Me: _____

Hang Tag Version: ☐   Tush Tag Version: ☐

Notes: _____

_____

_____

Current value: $95   2008 est. value: $1950

Teddy™ Brown

New Face & Old Face

	New Face	Old Face
Birthday:	11/28/95	Unknown
Introduced:	1/7/95	6/25/94
Retired Day:	10/1/97	1/7/95

Date I Got It: _____

Where I Got It: _____

I Paid: $ _____ or

Who Gave It to Me: _____

Hang Tag Version: ☐   Tush Tag Version: ☐

Notes: _____

Current value:
   $95 new
   $2750 old

2008 est. value:
   $750 new
   $3750 old

Teddy™ Cranberry

New Face & Old Face

	New Face	Old Face
Birthday:	Unknown	Unknown
Introduced:	1/7/95	6/25/94
Retired Day:	1/7/96	1/7/95

Date I Got It: _____

Where I Got It: _____

I Paid: $ _____ **or**

Who Gave It to Me: _____

Hang Tag Version: ☐   Tush Tag Version: ☐

Notes: _____

Current value: 2008 est. value:

  $1950 new $2750 new
  $1850 old $2650 old

Teddy™ Jade

New Face & Old Face

Bears

	New Face	Old Face
Birthday:	Unknown	Unknown
Introduced:	1/7/95	6/25/94
Retired Day:	1/7/96	1/7/95

Date I Got It: _____

Where I Got It: _____

I Paid: $ _____ **or**

Who Gave It to Me: _____

Hang Tag Version: ☐   Tush Tag Version: ☐

Notes: _____

Current value:
   $1950 new
   $1850 old

2008 est. value:
   $2750 new
   $2650 old

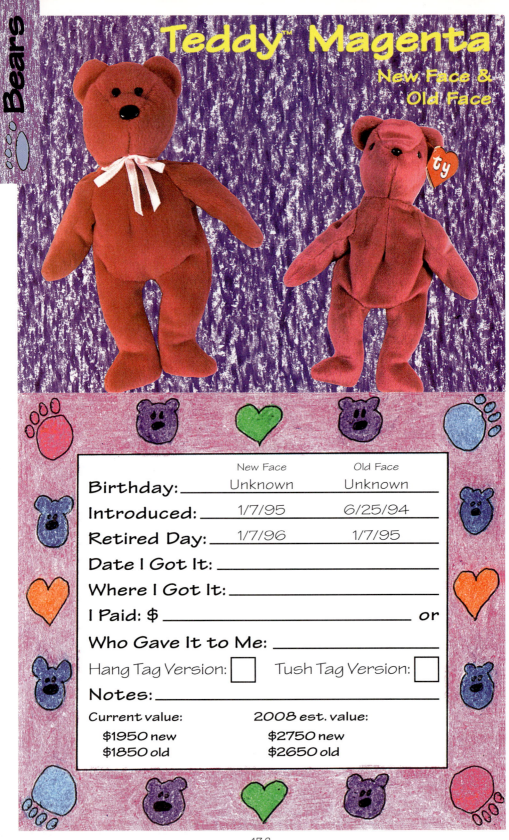

Teddy™ Magenta

New Face & Old Face

	New Face	Old Face
Birthday:	Unknown	Unknown
Introduced:	1/7/95	6/25/94
Retired Day:	1/7/96	1/7/95

Date I Got It: _____

Where I Got It: _____

I Paid: $ _____ **or**

Who Gave It to Me: _____

Hang Tag Version: ☐   Tush Tag Version: ☐

Notes: _____

Current value:
  $1950 new
  $1850 old

2008 est. value:
  $2750 new
  $2650 old

Teddy™ Teal

New Face & Old Face

	New Face	Old Face
Birthday:	Unknown	Unknown
Introduced:	1/7/95	6/25/94
Retired Day:	1/7/96	1/7/95

Date I Got It: _____

Where I Got It: _____

I Paid: $ _____ **or**

Who Gave It to Me: _____

Hang Tag Version: ☐   Tush Tag Version: ☐

Notes: _____

Current value: 2008 est. value:

  $1950 new $2750 new
  $1850 old $2650 old

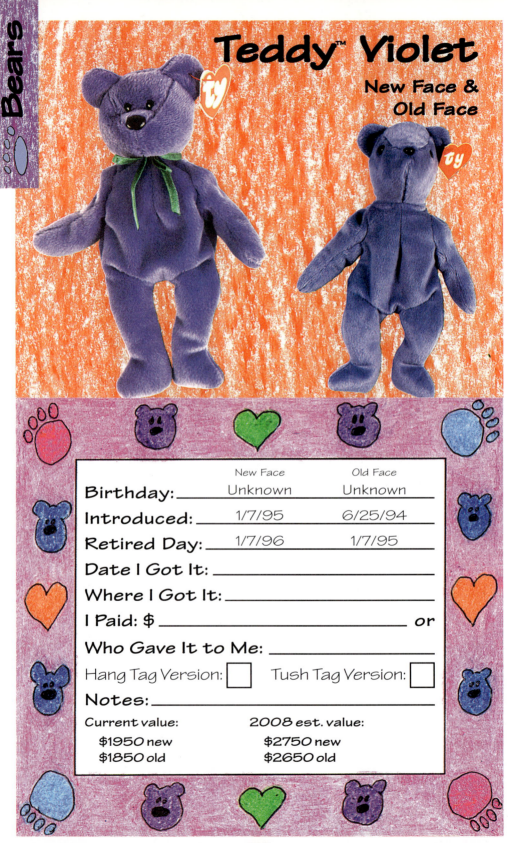

Teddy™ Violet

New Face & Old Face

	New Face	Old Face
Birthday:	Unknown	Unknown
Introduced:	1/7/95	6/25/94
Retired Day:	1/7/96	1/7/95

Date I Got It: _____

Where I Got It: _____

I Paid: $ _____ or

Who Gave It to Me: _____

Hang Tag Version: ☐   Tush Tag Version: ☐

Notes: _____

Current value: 2008 est. value:

$1950 new $2750 new

$1850 old $2650 old

Valentino™
the Bear

Birthday: February 14, 1994

Introduced: January 7, 1995

Retired Day: _____

Date I Got It: _____

Where I Got It: _____

I Paid: $ _____ **or**

Who Gave It to Me: _____

Hang Tag Version: ☐   Tush Tag Version: ☐

Notes: _____

_____

_____

Current value: **$30**   2008 est. value: **$750**

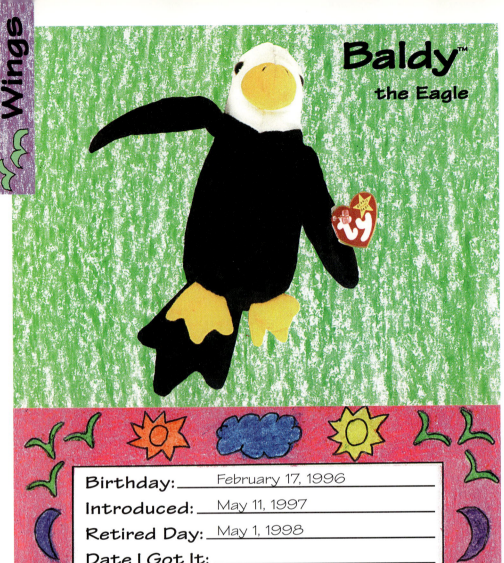

Baldy™
the Eagle

Birthday: ___February 17, 1996___

Introduced: ___May 11, 1997___

Retired Day: ___May 1, 1998___

Date I Got It: _____

Where I Got It: _____

I Paid: $ _____ or

Who Gave It to Me: _____

Hang Tag Version: ☐   Tush Tag Version: ☐

Notes: _____
_____
_____

Current value: $30   2008 est. value: $275

Batty™
the Bat

Wings

Birthday: _October 29, 1996_

Introduced: _October 1, 1997_

Retired Day: _____

Date I Got It: _____

Where I Got It: _____

I Paid: $ _____ or

Who Gave It to Me: _____

Hang Tag Version: ☐   Tush Tag Version: ☐

Notes: _____

_____

_____

Current value: $12   2008 est. value: $245

143

Bumble™
the Bee

Birthday: _Unknown_

Introduced: _June 3, 1995_

Retired Day: _June 15, 1996_

Date I Got It: _____

Where I Got It: _____

I Paid: $ _____ **or**

Who Gave It to Me: _____

Hang Tag Version: ☐   Tush Tag Version: ☐

Notes: _____
_____
_____

Current value: $ 600   2008 est. value: $ 1250

Caw™
the Crow

Birthday: Unknown

Introduced: June 3, 1995

Retired Day: June 15, 1996

Date I Got It: _____

Where I Got It: _____

I Paid: $ _____ or

Who Gave It to Me: _____

Hang Tag Version: ☐   Tush Tag Version: ☐

Notes: _____
_____
_____

Current value: **$695**   2008 est. value: **$1375**

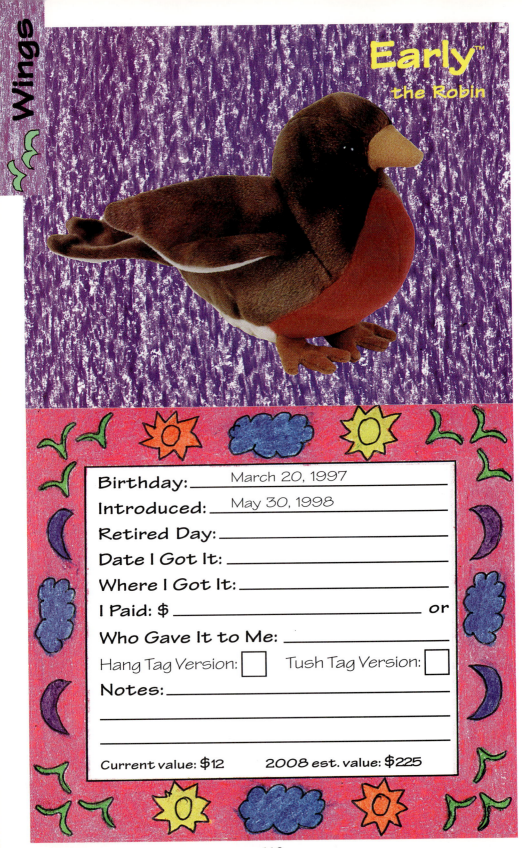

Early™
the Robin

Birthday: _____ March 20, 1997 _____

Introduced: _____ May 30, 1998 _____

Retired Day: _____

Date I Got It: _____

Where I Got It: _____

I Paid: $ _____ or

Who Gave It to Me: _____

Hang Tag Version: ☐   Tush Tag Version: ☐

Notes: _____

_____

_____

Current value: $12   2008 est. value: $225

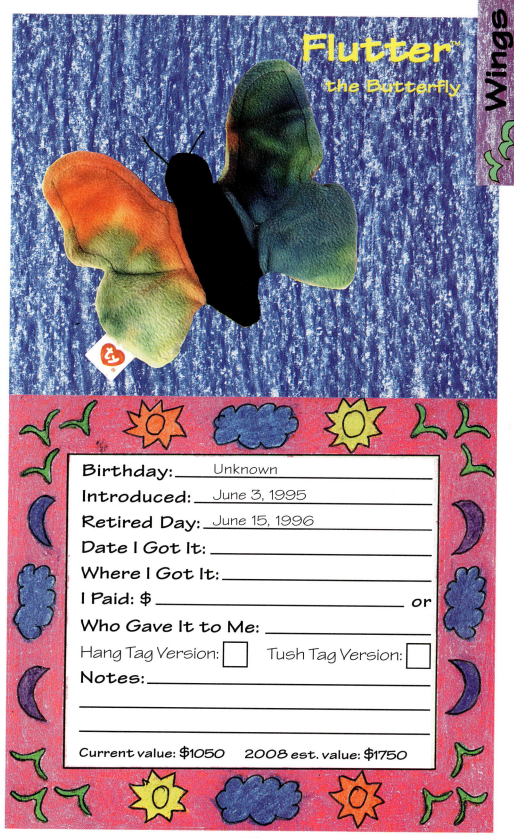

Flutter™
the Butterfly

Birthday: _Unknown_

Introduced: _June 3, 1995_

Retired Day: _June 15, 1996_

Date I Got It: _____

Where I Got It: _____

I Paid: $ _____ or

Who Gave It to Me: _____

Hang Tag Version: ☐   Tush Tag Version: ☐

Notes: _____

_____

_____

Current value: **$1050**   2008 est. value: **$1750**

Gobbles™
the Turkey

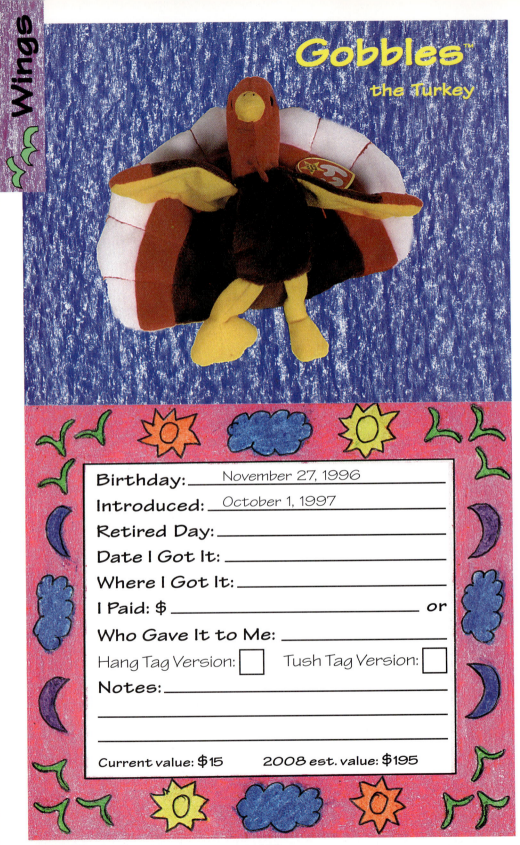

Birthday: _November 27, 1996_

Introduced: _October 1, 1997_

Retired Day: _____

Date I Got It: _____

Where I Got It: _____

I Paid: $ _____ or

Who Gave It to Me: _____

Hang Tag Version: ☐   Tush Tag Version: ☐

Notes: _____
_____
_____

Current value: $15   2008 est. value: $195

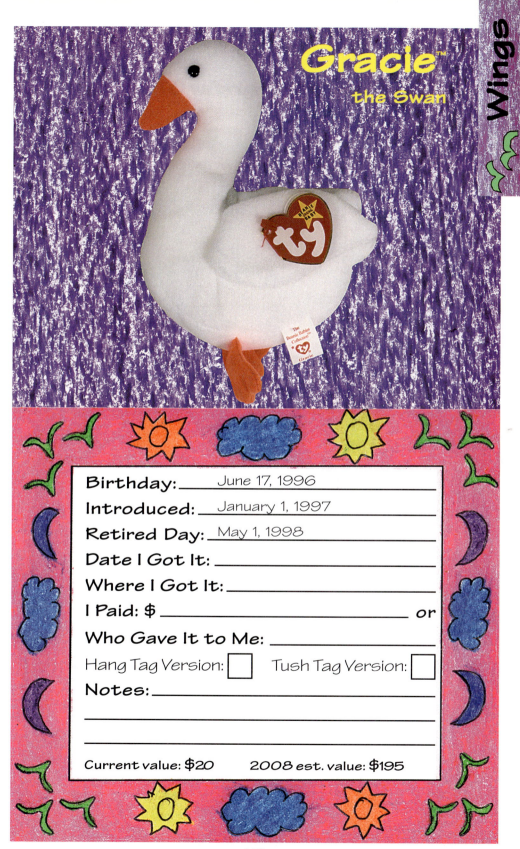

Gracie™
the Swan

Birthday: June 17, 1996

Introduced: January 1, 1997

Retired Day: May 1, 1998

Date I Got It: _____

Where I Got It: _____

I Paid: $ _____ **or**

Who Gave It to Me: _____

Hang Tag Version: ☐   Tush Tag Version: ☐

Notes: _____
_____
_____

Current value: $20   2008 est. value: $195

Hoot™
the Owl

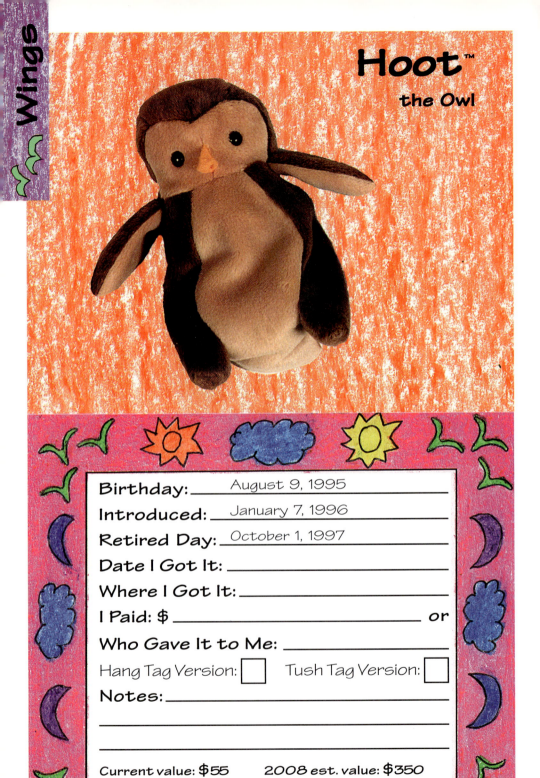

Birthday: August 9, 1995

Introduced: January 7, 1996

Retired Day: October 1, 1997

Date I Got It: _____

Where I Got It: _____

I Paid: $ _____ **or**

Who Gave It to Me: _____

Hang Tag Version: ☐   Tush Tag Version: ☐

Notes: _____
_____
_____

Current value: **$55**   2008 est. value: **$350**

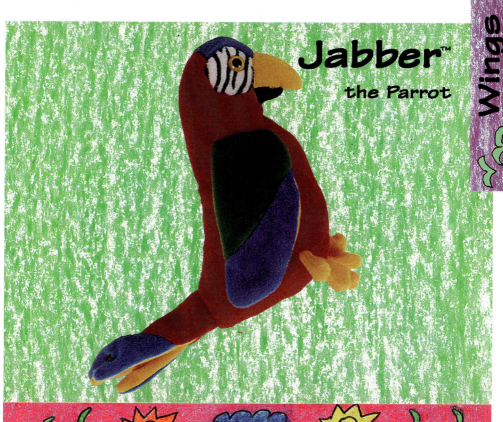

Jabber™
the Parrot

Birthday: _October 10, 1997_

Introduced: _May 30, 1998_

Retired Day: _____

Date I Got It: _____

Where I Got It: _____

I Paid: $ _____ **or**

Who Gave It to Me: _____

Hang Tag Version: ☐   Tush Tag Version: ☐

Notes: _____

_____

_____

Current value: $15   2008 est. value: $275

Wings

Jake™
the Mallard Duck

Birthday: _April 16, 1997_

Introduced: _May 30, 1998_

Retired Day: _____

Date I Got It: _____

Where I Got It: _____

I Paid: $ _____ or

Who Gave It to Me: _____

Hang Tag Version: ☐ Tush Tag Version: ☐

Notes: _____

_____

_____

Current value: $12   2008 est. value: $250

Kiwi™
the Toucan

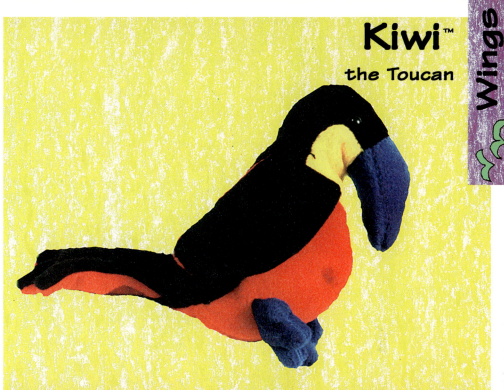

Birthday: September 16, 1995

Introduced: June 3, 1995

Retired Day: January 1, 1997

Date I Got It: _____

Where I Got It: _____

I Paid: $ _____ **or**

Who Gave It to Me: _____

Hang Tag Version: ☐   Tush Tag Version: ☐

Notes: _____
_____
_____

Current value: $195   2008 est. value: $650

Kuku™
the Cockatoo

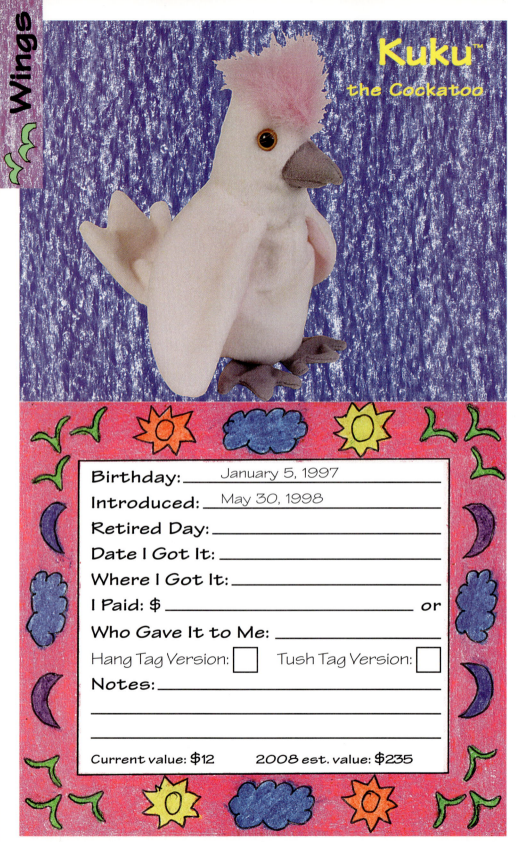

Birthday: January 5, 1997

Introduced: May 30, 1998

Retired Day: _____

Date I Got It: _____

Where I Got It: _____

I Paid: $ _____ **or**

Who Gave It to Me: _____

Hang Tag Version: ☐   Tush Tag Version: ☐

Notes: _____
_____
_____

Current value: **$12**   2008 est. value: **$235**

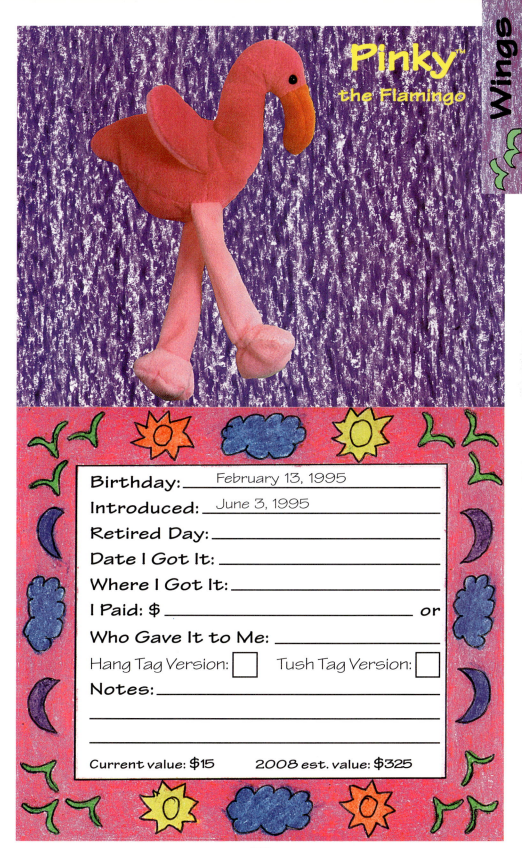

Pinky™
the Flamingo

Wings

Birthday: _February 13, 1995_

Introduced: _June 3, 1995_

Retired Day: _____

Date I Got It: _____

Where I Got It: _____

I Paid: $ _____ **or**

Who Gave It to Me: _____

Hang Tag Version: ☐   Tush Tag Version: ☐

Notes: _____
_____
_____

Current value: **$15**   2008 est. value: **$325**

Puffer™
the Puffin

Birthday: _November 3, 1997_

Introduced: _December 31, 1997_

Retired Day: _____

Date I Got It: _____

Where I Got It: _____

I Paid: $ _____ **or**

Who Gave It to Me: _____

Hang Tag Version: ☐   Tush Tag Version: ☐

Notes: _____
_____
_____

Current value: $12   2008 est. value: $225

Radar™
the Bat

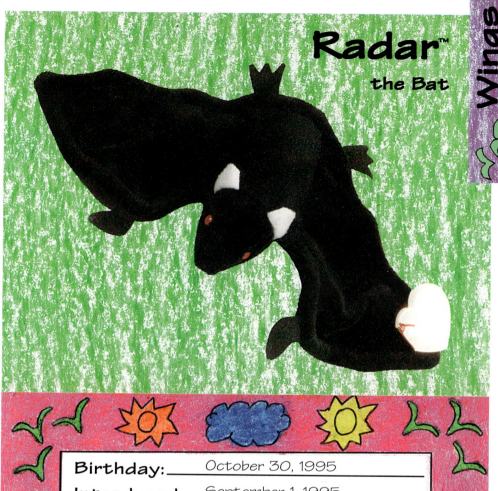

Birthday: October 30, 1995

Introduced: September 1, 1995

Retired Day: May 11, 1997

Date I Got It: _____

Where I Got It: _____

I Paid: $ _____ **or**

Who Gave It to Me: _____

Hang Tag Version: ☐   Tush Tag Version: ☐

Notes: _____

_____

_____

Current value: $175   2008 est. value: $450

Rocket™
the Blue Jay

Birthday: March 12, 1997

Introduced: May 30, 1998

Retired Day: _____

Date I Got It: _____

Where I Got It: _____

I Paid: $ _____ or

Who Gave It to Me: _____

Hang Tag Version: ☐   Tush Tag Version: ☐

Notes: _____
_____
_____

Current value: $15   2008 est. value: $295

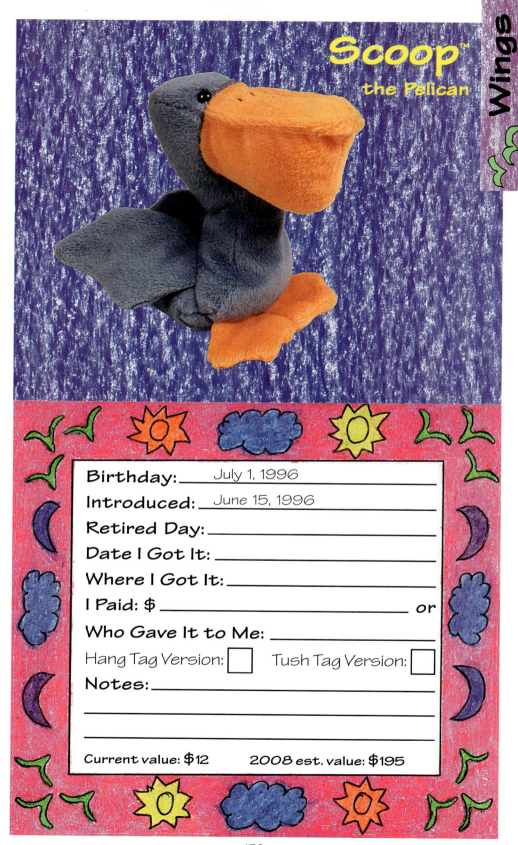

Scoop™
the Pelican

Wings

Birthday: July 1, 1996

Introduced: June 15, 1996

Retired Day: _____

Date I Got It: _____

Where I Got It: _____

I Paid: $ _____ **or**

Who Gave It to Me: _____

Hang Tag Version: ☐   Tush Tag Version: ☐

Notes: _____

_____

_____

Current value: $12   2008 est. value: $195

159

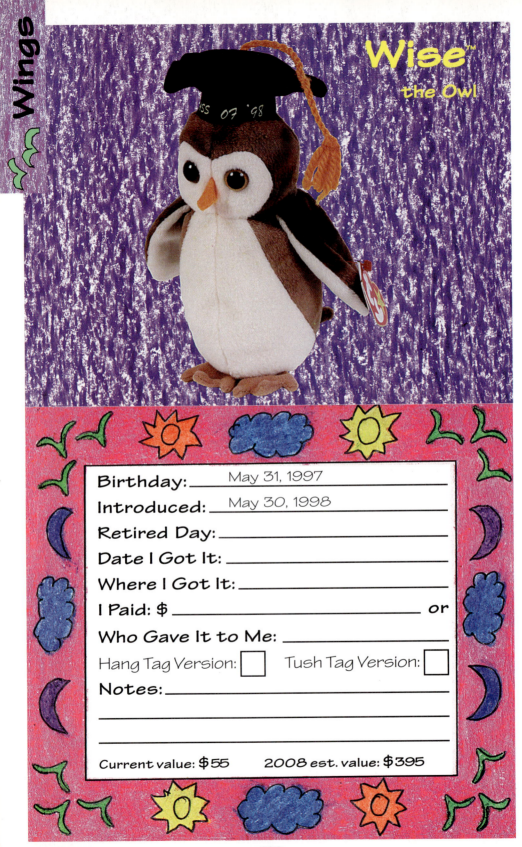

Wise™
the Owl

Birthday: _May 31, 1997_

Introduced: _May 30, 1998_

Retired Day: _____

Date I Got It: _____

Where I Got It: _____

I Paid: $ _____ **or**

Who Gave It to Me: _____

Hang Tag Version: ☐   Tush Tag Version: ☐

Notes: _____
_____
_____

Current value: $55   2008 est. value: $395

Magic™
the Dragon

Birthday: September 5, 1995

Introduced: June 3, 1995

Retired Day: December 31, 1997

Date I Got It: _____

Where I Got It: _____

I Paid: $ _____ or

Who Gave It to Me: _____

Hang Tag Version: ☐   Tush Tag Version: ☐

Notes: _____
_____
_____

Current value: $55   2008 est. value: $450

Mystic™

the Unicorn
with iridescent horn &
with brown horn

	iridescent	brown
Birthday:	5/21/94	5/21/94
Introduced:	10/23/97	6/25/94
Retired Day:		10/23/97

Date I Got It: _____

Where I Got It: _____

I Paid: $ _____ **or**

Who Gave It to Me: _____

Hang Tag Version: ☐   Tush Tag Version: ☐

Notes: _____

Current value:
  $15 iridescent
  $40 brown

2008 est. value:
  $255 iridescent
  $350 brown

Snowball™

the Snowman

Birthday: _December 22, 1996_

Introduced: _October 1, 1997_

Retired Day: _December 31, 1997_

Date I Got It: _____

Where I Got It: _____

I Paid: $ _____ or

Who Gave It to Me: _____

Hang Tag Version: ☐   Tush Tag Version: ☐

Notes: _____

_____

_____

Current value: **$45**   2008 est. value: **$450**

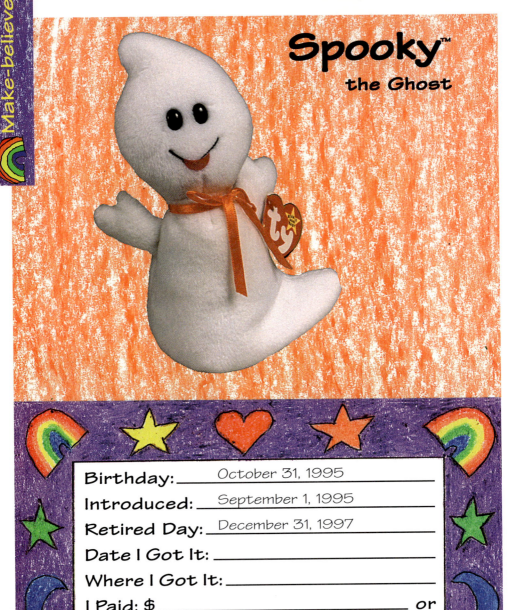

Spooky™
the Ghost

Birthday: _October 31, 1995_

Introduced: _September 1, 1995_

Retired Day: _December 31, 1997_

Date I Got It: _____

Where I Got It: _____

I Paid: $ _____ **or**

Who Gave It to Me: _____

Hang Tag Version: ☐   Tush Tag Version: ☐

Notes: _____
_____
_____

Current value: **$45**   2008 est. value: **$450**

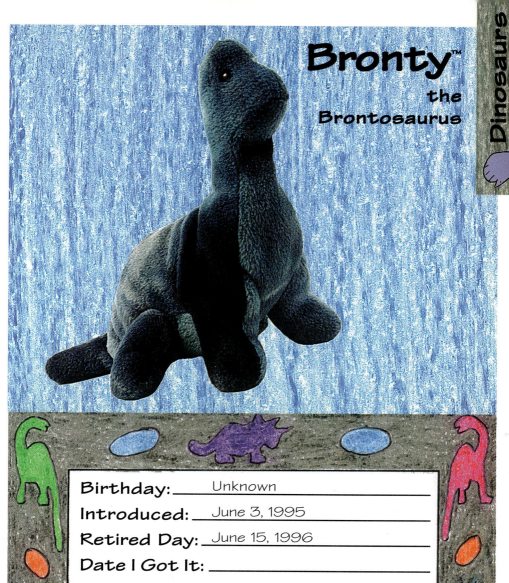

Bronty™

the
Brontosaurus

Birthday: _Unknown_

Introduced: _June 3, 1995_

Retired Day: _June 15, 1996_

Date I Got It: _____

Where I Got It: _____

I Paid: $ _____ **or**

Who Gave It to Me: _____

Hang Tag Version: ☐   Tush Tag Version: ☐

Notes: _____
_____
_____

Current value: $1100   2008 est. value: $2150

Rex™
the Tyrannosaurus

Birthday: _Unknown_

Introduced: _June 3, 1995_

Retired Day: _June 15, 1996_

Date I Got It: _____

Where I Got It: _____

I Paid: $ _____ **or**

Who Gave It to Me: _____

Hang Tag Version: ☐ Tush Tag Version: ☐

Notes: _____
_____
_____

Current value: $1000   2008 est. value: $2100

Steg™
the Stegosaurus

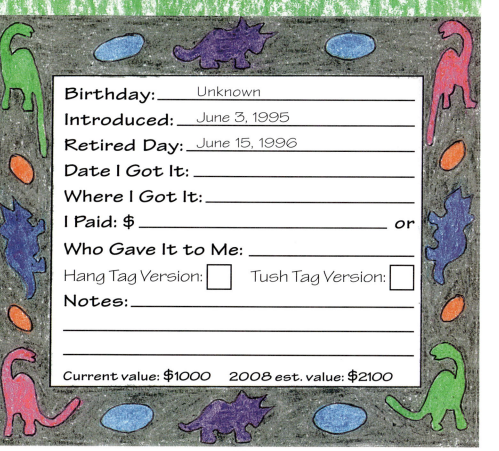

Birthday: _Unknown_

Introduced: _June 3, 1995_

Retired Day: _June 15, 1996_

Date I Got It: _____

Where I Got It: _____

I Paid: $ _____ **or**

Who Gave It to Me: _____

Hang Tag Version: ☐   Tush Tag Version: ☐

Notes: _____
_____
_____

Current value: $1000   2008 est. value: $2100

Britannia™
the Bear

Birthday: _December 15, 1997_

Introduced: _December 31, 1997_

Retired Day: _____

Date I Got It: _____

Where I Got It: _____

I Paid: $ _____ **or**

Who Gave It to Me: _____

Hang Tag Version: ☐   Tush Tag Version: ☐

Notes: _____
_____
_____

Current value: $500   2008 est. value: $2250

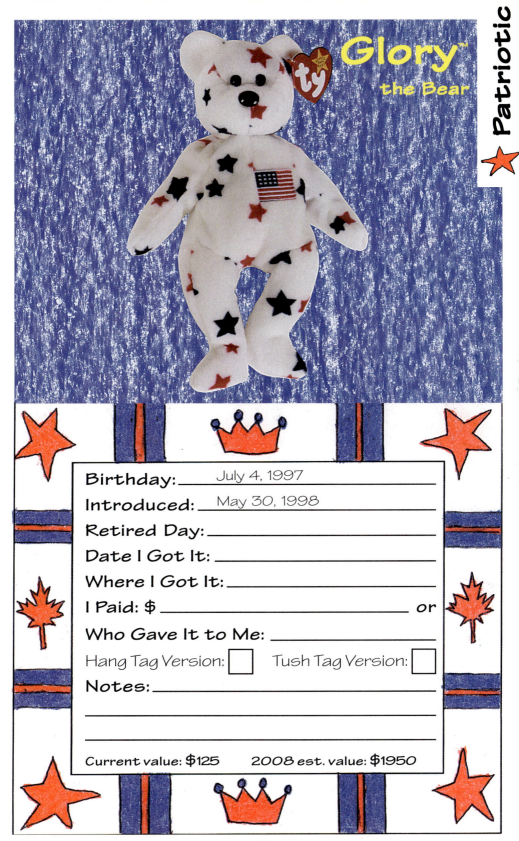

Glory
the Bear

Birthday: _July 4, 1997_

Introduced: _May 30, 1998_

Retired Day: _____

Date I Got It: _____

Where I Got It: _____

I Paid: $ _____ **or**

Who Gave It to Me: _____

Hang Tag Version: ☐   Tush Tag Version: ☐

Notes: _____
_____
_____

Current value: **$125**   2008 est. value: **$1950**

Lefty™
the Donkey

Birthday: _July 4, 1996_

Introduced: _June 15, 1996_

Retired Day: _January 1, 1997_

Date I Got It: _____

Where I Got It: _____

I Paid: $ _____ or

Who Gave It to Me: _____

Hang Tag Version: ☐   Tush Tag Version: ☐

Notes: _____

_____

_____

Current value: $325   2008 est. value: $2450

Libearty™
the Bear

Birthday: _Summer 1996_

Introduced: _June 15, 1996_

Retired Day: _January 1, 1997_

Date I Got It: _____

Where I Got It: _____

I Paid: $ _____ **or**

Who Gave It to Me: _____

Hang Tag Version: ☐   Tush Tag Version: ☐

Notes: _____
_____
_____

Current value: $450   2008 est. value: $2200

Maple™
the Bear

Birthday: _July 1, 1996_

Introduced: _January 1, 1997_

Retired Day: _____

Date I Got It: _____

Where I Got It: _____

I Paid: $ _____ **or**

Who Gave It to Me: _____

Hang Tag Version: ☐   Tush Tag Version: ☐

Notes: _____
_____
_____

Current value: $250   2008 est. value: $2250

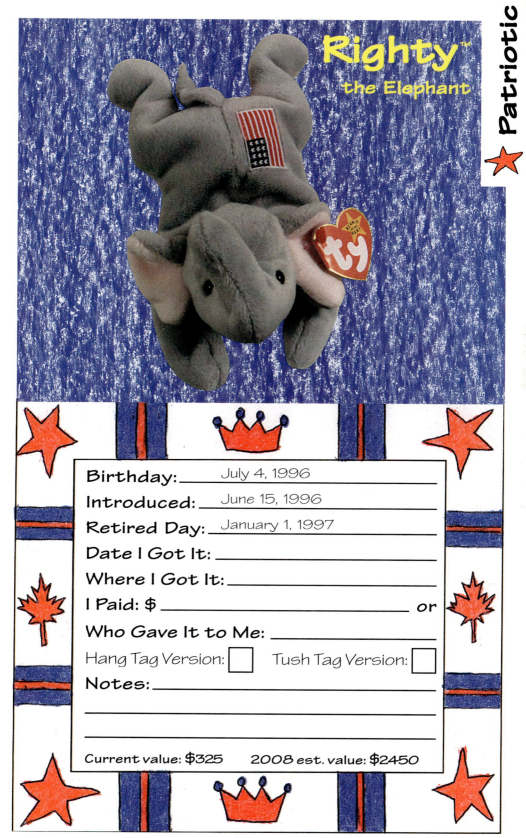

Righty™
the Elephant

Birthday: _____ July 4, 1996 _____

Introduced: _____ June 15, 1996 _____

Retired Day: _____ January 1, 1997 _____

Date I Got It: _____

Where I Got It: _____

I Paid: $ _____ or

Who Gave It to Me: _____

Hang Tag Version: ☐   Tush Tag Version: ☐

Notes: _____
_____
_____

Current value: $325   2008 est. value: $2450

Teenie Beanies are official Ty animals made in miniature size to match a larger Beanie Baby. The fabric is felt-like and different from the plush fabric of a Beanie Baby.

The original 10 McDonald's Teenie Beanies were first introduced in Happy Meals in April 1997. It became the most successful Happy Meal promotion in McDonald's history. The original promotion was scheduled to run for 5 weeks — from April 11, 1997 until May 16, 1997. Collectors went nuts and the 100 million Teenie Beanies were sold out around the country in 2 weeks. McDonald's was forced to end the event early.

The second time Ty & McDonald's tried this joint venture they made 20 million of each Teenie Beanie (12 different ones this time) for a total of 240 million Teenies. That's about one for every person in the U.S.! Some towns had enough Teenies for the entire 4 weeks of this promotion — May 22, 1998 to June 18, 1998 — and some ran out early. Values listed are for Teenies in their original plastic bags with perfect tags.

Teenie Beanie Babies™, April 11-25, 1997

#1 Patti

Date I Got It:_____

Where I Got It: _____

I Paid: $: _____ or

Who Gave It to Me: _____

Notes: _____

Current value: $45   2008 est. value: $75

#2 Pinky

Date I Got It:_____

Where I Got It: _____

I Paid: $: _____ or

Who Gave It to Me: _____

Notes: _____

Current value: $50   2008 est. value: $80

Teenie Beanie Babies™, April 11-25, 1997

#3 Chops

Date I Got It:_____

Where I Got It: _____

I Paid: $: _____ or

Who Gave It to Me: _____

Notes: _____

Current value: $40   2008 est. value: $70

#4 Chocolate

Date I Got It:_____

Where I Got It: _____

I Paid: $: _____ or

Who Gave It to Me: _____

Notes: _____

Current value: $35   2008 est. value: $65

#5 Goldie

Date I Got It:_____

Where I Got It: _____

I Paid: $: _____ or

Who Gave It to Me: _____

Notes: _____

Current value: $35   2008 est. value: $75

#6 Speedy

Date I Got It:_____

Where I Got It: _____

I Paid: $: _____ or

Who Gave It to Me: _____

Notes: _____

Current value: $30   2008 est. value: $60

#7 Seamore

Date I Got It:_____

Where I Got It: _____

I Paid: $: _____ or

Who Gave It to Me: _____

Notes: _____

Current value: $35   2008 est. value: $65

#8 Snort

Date I Got It:_____

Where I Got It: _____

I Paid: $: _____ or

Who Gave It to Me: _____

Notes: _____

Current value: $25   2008 est. value: $55

#9 Quacks

Date I Got It:_____

Where I Got It: _____

I Paid: $: _____ or

Who Gave It to Me: _____

Notes: _____

Current value: $25   2008 est. value: $55

#10 Lizz

Date I Got It:_____

Where I Got It: _____

I Paid: $: _____ or

Who Gave It to Me: _____

Notes: _____

Current value: $25   2008 est. value: $55

#1 Doby

Date I Got It:_____

Where I Got It: _____

I Paid: $: _____ or

Who Gave It to Me: _____

Notes: _____

Current value: $25   2008 est. value: $55

#2 Bongo

Date I Got It:_____

Where I Got It: _____

I Paid: $: _____ or

Who Gave It to Me: _____

Notes: _____

Current value: $25   2008 est. value: $55

#3 Twigs

Date I Got It:_____

Where I Got It: _____

I Paid: $: _____ or

Who Gave It to Me: _____

Notes: _____

Current value: $25   2008 est. value: $55

#4 Inch

Date I Got It:_____

Where I Got It: _____

I Paid: $: _____ or

Who Gave It to Me: _____

Notes: _____

Current value: $22   2008 est. value: $50

#5 Pinchers

Date I Got It:_____

Where I Got It: _____

I Paid: $: _____ or

Who Gave It to Me: _____

Notes: _____

Current value: $22   2008 est. value: $50

#6 Happy

Date I Got It:_____

Where I Got It: _____

I Paid: $: _____ or

Who Gave It to Me: _____

Notes: _____

Current value: $22   2008 est. value: $50

#7 Mel

Date I Got It:_____

Where I Got It: _____

I Paid: $: _____ or

Who Gave It to Me: _____

Notes: _____

Current value: $20   2008 est. value: $45

#8 Scoop

Date I Got It:_____

Where I Got It: _____

I Paid: $: _____ or

Who Gave It to Me: _____

Notes: _____

Current value: $20   2008 est. value: $45

#9 Bones

Date I Got It:_____

Where I Got It: _____

I Paid: $: _____ or

Who Gave It to Me: _____

Notes: _____

Current value: $25   2008 est. value: $55

#10 Zip

Date I Got It:_____

Where I Got It: _____

I Paid: $: _____ or

Who Gave It to Me: _____

Notes: _____

Current value: $22   2008 est. value: $50

#11 Waddle

Date I Got It:_____

Where I Got It: _____

I Paid: $: _____ or

Who Gave It to Me: _____

Notes: _____

Current value: $22   2008 est. value: $50

#12 Peanut

Date I Got It:_____

Where I Got It: _____

I Paid: $: _____ or

Who Gave It to Me: _____

Notes: _____

Current value: $25   2008 est. value: $55

Ten Great Ways to Display or Store Your Collection

1. Get a plastic shoe rack that hangs over the back of a door. Beanies look super cute peeking out of each pocket.

2. Get some of the plastic cube containers that most Beanie dealers sell. They keep your Beanies from getting dusty and they look really neat all stacked up in cool displays.

3. Do you have any shelves in your room? Beanies look awesome all piled up together on a shelf.

4. To keep Beanies clean and safe, get one of those large, flat plastic containers that slide under a bed. Your mom will love this idea and it will keep your Beanies neat and tidy and close by while you sleep.

5. Plastic milk crates are neat to stack, and each one makes a great house for a bunch of Beanies.

6. Serious collectors keep each Beanie in its own large, sealed baggie. These keep the Beanies clean and the tags safe.

7. Ever see those collapsible mesh hanging racks for use in the kitchen? They are awesome to hang in your room with a pile of Beanies on each level.

8. Have any baskets with handles around your house? Tie a cute ribbon on each one and hang from hooks in your ceiling. Stagger them at different levels. Let the dogs and cats peek over the edge of one and the teddy bears over another.

9. Baskets also look cute on a shelf or table. Each basket can hold a different grouping, for example one for sea life and another for teddy bears.

10. Do you take your Beanies to your friends' houses to play? Borrow a small cooler with a handle from your parents. It's a safe and fun way to carry your Beanies — and they won't get too hot!

Beanie Baby Checklist

Dogs

	Want It	Got It
Bernie	✓	✓
Bones	✓	
Bruno		✓
Doby		✓
Dotty		✓
Fetch	✓	
Gigi	✓	✓
Nanook	✓	✓
Pugsly	✓	✓
Rover		✓
Scottie	✓	✓
Sparky		✓
Spot	✓	
Spot – no spot	✓	
Spunky	✓	✓
Tracker		✓
Tuffy	✓	
Weenie	✓	✓
Wrinkles	✓	

Cats

	Want It	Got It
Chip	✓	
Flip	✓	
Nip – white paws	✓	
Nip – all gold	✓	
Nip – white face	✓	
Pounce		✓
Prance		✓
Snip		✓

	Want It	Got It
Zip – white paws	✓	
Zip – all black	✓	
Zip – white face	✓	

Farm

	Want It	Got It
Bessie		
Chops		✓
Daisy		✓
Derby – with star		
Derby – without star	✓	
Fleece		✓
Grunt	✓	
Quackers – wingless		
Quackers – with wings	✓	✓
Snort		✓
Squealer	✓	✓
Strut	✓	
Doodle	✓	
Tabasco	✓	

Forest

	Want It	Got It
Bucky	✓	
Chocolate		✓
Ears		✓
Floppity		✓
Hippity	✓	✓
Hoppity		✓
Legs		✓
Nuts		✓
Ringo		✓
Sly – brown belly	✓	

Beanie Baby Checklist

	Want It	Got It
Sly – white belly		✓
Smoochy		✓
Stinky		✓
Trap	✓	
Whisper		✓

Jungle

	Want It	Got It
Ants	✓	
Blizzard	✓	
Bongo – brown tail	✓	
Bongo – tan tail	✓	
Nana	✓	
Congo	✓	
Freckles		✓
Happy – gray	✓	
Happy – lavender	✓	
Humphrey	✓	
Mel		✓
Peanut – royal blue	✓	✓
Peanut – light blue	✓	✓
Pouch		✓
Roary		✓
Spike		✓
Stretch		✓
Stripes – thin stripes	✓	
Stripes – wide stripes	✓	
Twigs	✓	
Velvet		✓
Ziggy	✓	

Dinosaurs

	Want It	Got It
Bronty	✓	
Rex	✓	
Steg	✓	

Crawlers

	Want It	Got It
Ally	✓	
Hissy	✓	
Iggy		✓
Inch – felt		
Inch – yarn		✓
Lizzy – tie-dyed		✓
Lizzy – blue		
Lucky – felt		
Lucky – printed		
Rainbow w/o tongue	✓	
Rainbow w/ tongue	✓	
Slither	✓	
Speedy	✓	
Spinner	✓	
Stinger	✓	
Tank – without shell	✓	
Tank – with shell	✓	
Web	✓	

Beanie Baby Checklist

	Want It	Got It

⭐ Patriotic

	Want It	Got It
Britannia	✓	☐
Glory	✓	☐
Lefty	✓	☐
Libearty	✓	☐
Maple	✓	☐
Righty	✓	☐

🐟 Sea

	Want It	Got It
Bubbles	✓	☐
Claude	✓	☐
Coral	✓	☐
Crunch	✓	☐
Digger – orange	✓	☐
Digger – red	✓	☐
Echo	✓	☐
Flash	☐	☐
Goldie	✓	☐
Inky – pink	✓	☐
Inky – tan without mouth	☐	☐
Inky – tan with mouth	✓	☐
Jolly	✓	☐
Manny	✓	☐
Patti – maroon	✓	☐
Patti – magenta	✓	☐
Pinchers	☐	✓
Seamore	✓	☐
Seaweed	✓	☐
Splash	✓	☐
Sting	✓	☐
Tusk	✓	☐

	Want It	Got It
Waddle	☐	✓
Waves	☐	✓

🐾 Bears

	Want It	Got It
1997 Teddy	✓	☐
Blackie	✓	☐
Brownie	✓	☐
Chilly	✓	☐
Clubby	✓	✓
Cubbie	✓	☐
Curly	✓	✓
Erin	☐	✓
Fortune	✓	✓
Garcia	✓	☐
Peace	☐	✓
Peking	✓	☐
Princess	☐	✓
Teddy Brown new	☐	☐
Teddy Brown old	✓	☐
Teddy Cranberry new	✓	☐
Teddy Cranberry old	✓	☐
Teddy Jade new	✓	☐
Teddy Jade old	✓	☐
Teddy Magenta new	✓	☐
Teddy Magenta old	✓	☐
Teddy Teal new	✓	☐
Teddy Teal old	✓	☐
Teddy Violet new	✓	☐
Teddy Violet old	✓	✓
Valentino	☐	✓

Beanie Baby Checklist

	Want It	Got It
Wings		
Baldy	☑	☐
Batty	☑	☐
Bumble	☑	☐
Caw	☑	☐
Early	☐	☑
Flutter	☑	☐
Gobbles	☑	☐
Gracie	☑	☐
Hoot	☑	☐
Jabber	☐	☑
Jake	☑	☐
Kiwi	☑	☐
Kuku	☐	☐
Pinky	☐	☑
Puffer	☐	☑
Radar	☑	☐
Rocket	☐	☑
Scoop	☐	☑
Wise	☑	☐
Make-believe		
Magic	☐	☐
Mystic – iridescent	☐	☑
Mystic – brown	☐	☑
Snowball	☐	☐
Spooky	☐	☐

	Want It	Got It
Teenie Beanies 1997		
Patti	☐	☑
Pinky	☐	☐
Chops	☑	☐
Chocolate	☐	☑
Goldie	☐	☑
Speedy	☐	☑
Seamore	☐	☑
Snort	☐	☑
Quacks	☑	☐
Lizz	☑	☐
Teenie Beanies 1998		
Doby	☑	☑
Bongo	☐	☐
Twigs	☐	☐
Inch	☐	☐
Pinchers	☐	☑
Happy	☐	☐
Mel	☐	☐
Scoop	☐	☐
Bones	☐	☐
Zip	☑	☐
Waddle	☑	☑
Peanut	☑	☐

Index of Beanie Babies®

New Additions
and Updates
to the

Beanie Babies

Collection®

Canyon™
the Cougar

Birthday: _May 29, 1998_

Introduced: _September 30, 1998_

Retired Day: _____

Date I Got It: _____

Where I Got It: _____

I Paid: $ _____ or

Who Gave It to Me: _____

Hang Tag Version: ☐   Tush Tag Version: ☐

Notes: _____

_____

_____

Current value: $8   2008 est. value: $150

Roam™

the Buffalo

Forest

Birthday: September 27, 1998

Introduced: September 30, 1998

Retired Day: _____

Date I Got It: _____

Where I Got It: _____

I Paid: $ _____ **or**

Who Gave It to Me: _____

Hang Tag Version: ☐   Tush Tag Version: ☐

Notes: _____
_____
_____

Current value: $10   2008 est. value: $165

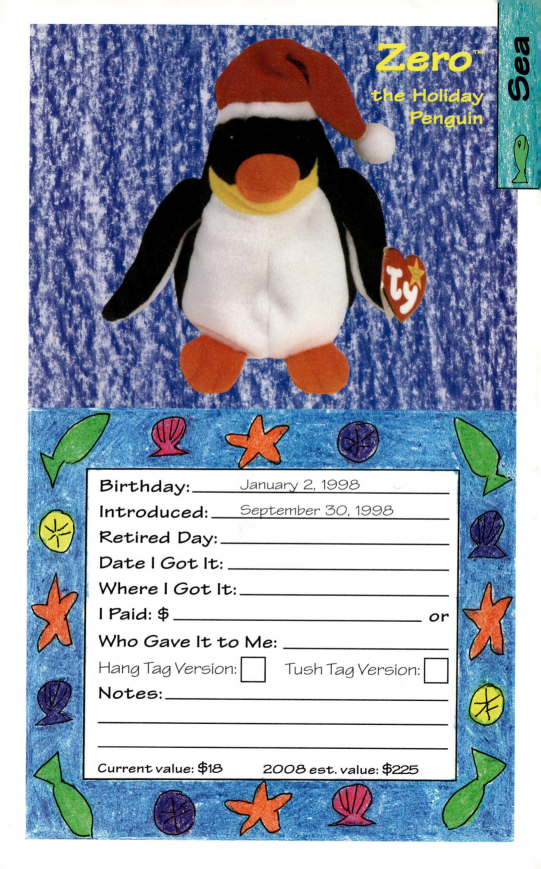

Zero™
the Holiday
Penguin

Sea

Birthday: _____ January 2, 1998 _____

Introduced: _____ September 30, 1998 _____

Retired Day: _____

Date I Got It: _____

Where I Got It: _____

I Paid: $ _____ or

Who Gave It to Me: _____

Hang Tag Version: ☐   Tush Tag Version: ☐

Notes: _____
_____
_____

Current value: $18   2008 est. value: $225

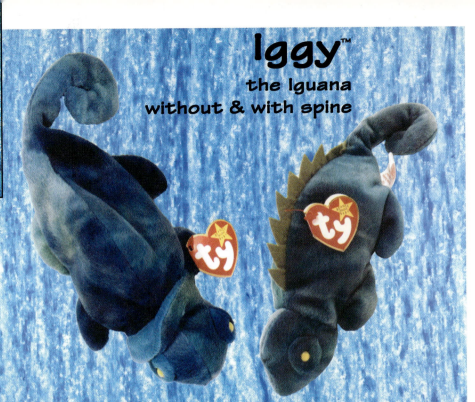

Iggy™
the Iguana
without & with spine

	without spine	with spine
Birthday:	8/12/97	8/12/97
Introduced:	12/31/97	August 1998
Retired Day:	August 1998	

Date I Got It: _____

Where I Got It: _____

I Paid: $ _____ **or**

Who Gave It to Me: _____

Hang Tag Version: ☐   **Tush Tag Version:** ☐

Notes: _____

Current value: 2008 est. value:
  $15 without spine $325 without spine
  $10 with spine $250 with spine

Rainbow™

the Chameleon
without spine

Birthday: _October 14, 1997_

Introduced: _August 1998_

Retired Day: _____

Date I Got It: _____

Where I Got It: _____

I Paid: $ _____ **or**

Who Gave It to Me: _____

Hang Tag Version: ☐   Tush Tag Version: ☐

Notes: _____
_____
_____

Current value: **$10**   2008 est. value: **$225**

1998 Teddy™

Holiday Bear

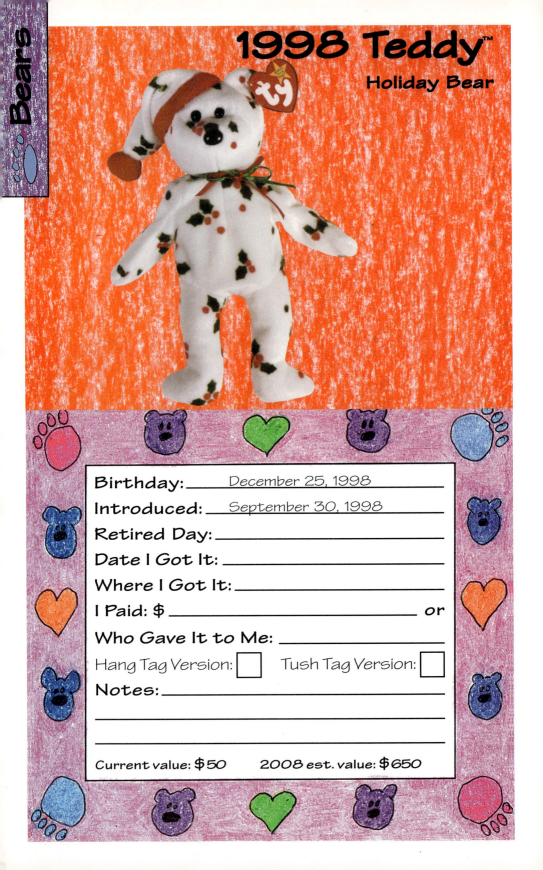

Birthday: _December 25, 1998_

Introduced: _September 30, 1998_

Retired Day: _____

Date I Got It: _____

Where I Got It: _____

I Paid: $ _____ or

Who Gave It to Me: _____

Hang Tag Version: ☐   Tush Tag Version: ☐

Notes: _____

_____

_____

Current value: $50   2008 est. value: $650

Halo™

the Angel Bear

Bears

Birthday: August 31, 1998

Introduced: September 30, 1998

Retired Day: _____

Date I Got It: _____

Where I Got It: _____

I Paid: $ _____ or

Who Gave It to Me: _____

Hang Tag Version: ☐   Tush Tag Version: ☐

Notes: _____
_____
_____

Current value: **$45**   2008 est. value: **$575**

Beak™

the Kiwi Bird

Birthday: February 3, 1998

Introduced: September 30, 1998

Retired Day: _____

Date I Got It: _____

Where I Got It: _____

I Paid: $ _____ **or**

Who Gave It to Me: _____

Hang Tag Version: ☐   Tush Tag Version: ☐

Notes: _____
_____
_____

Current value: $8   2008 est. value: $195

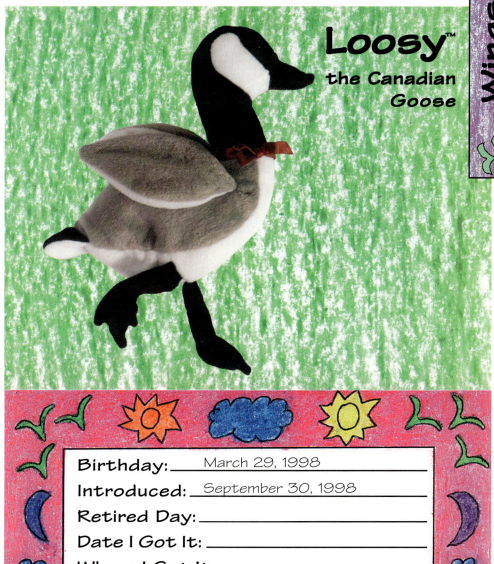

Loosy™
the Canadian Goose

Wings

Birthday: _March 29, 1998_

Introduced: _September 30, 1998_

Retired Day: _____

Date I Got It: _____

Where I Got It: _____

I Paid: $ _____ or

Who Gave It to Me: _____

Hang Tag Version: ☐   Tush Tag Version: ☐

Notes: _____

_____

_____

Current value: $8   2008 est. value: $225

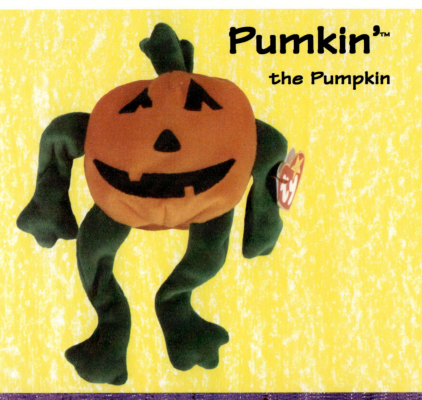

Pumkin'™

the Pumpkin

Make-believe

Make-believe

Birthday: _October 31, 1998_

Introduced: _September 30, 1998_

Retired Day: _____

Date I Got It: _____

Where I Got It: _____

I Paid: $ _____ **or**

Who Gave It to Me: _____

Hang Tag Version: ☐   Tush Tag Version: ☐

Notes: _____
_____
_____

Current value: $15   2008 est. value: $275

Santa™

Birthday: _December 6, 1998_

Introduced: _September 30, 1998_

Retired Day: _____

Date I Got It: _____

Where I Got It: _____

I Paid: $ _____ **or**

Who Gave It to Me: _____

Hang Tag Version: ☐   Tush Tag Version: ☐

Notes: _____
_____
_____

Current value: **$25**   2008 est. value: **$375**

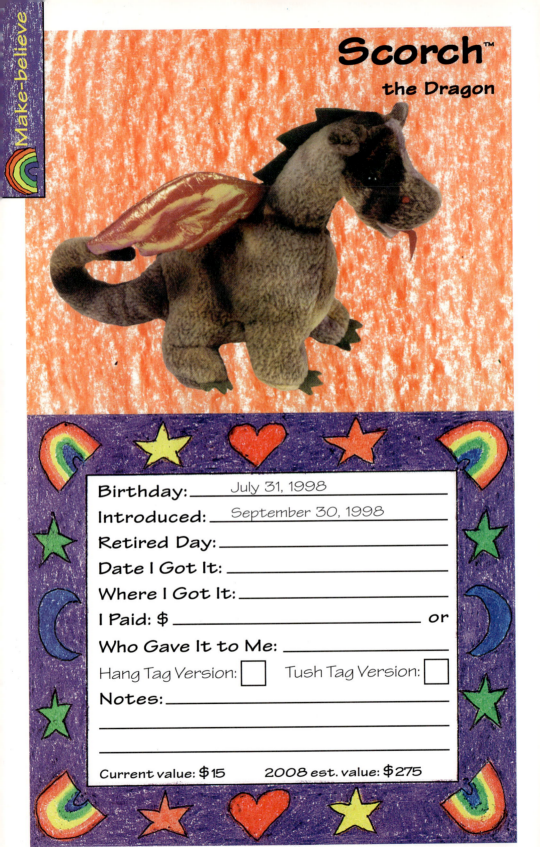

Make-believe

Scorch™
the Dragon

Birthday: _July 31, 1998_

Introduced: _September 30, 1998_

Retired Day: _____

Date I Got It: _____

Where I Got It: _____

I Paid: $ _____ **or**

Who Gave It to Me: _____

Hang Tag Version: ☐   Tush Tag Version: ☐

Notes: _____
_____
_____

Current value: $15   2008 est. value: $275